THE HUMAN COST OF GLOBALIZATION

When KenSa, LLC, a manufacturer of electrical systems for the auto industry, left Michigan for a dusty factory town in Mexico, the new work force south of the border rejoiced. But within a few years the Mexican employees were replaced by a cheaper labor force in Honduras. Then, before the permanent facility there was complete, KenSa moved again—to China, where workers lined up for jobs paying 45 cents an hour. Ironically, when government financing fell through, the Chinese workers were laid off too.

Driven Abroad reveals the hidden side of outsourcing, showing how workers around the world are being laid off in a global game of leapfrog that has redefined business from Brooklyn to Beijing.

The first writer/photographer team ever allowed unlimited access to workplaces and corporate suites for a book on outsourcing, Ron French and Max Ortiz have written an unforgettable story about the tragic consequences of labor globalization in America and the Third World. A must-read for everyone who cares about the future of labor, this book is for workers, corporate executives, politicians, community leaders and students of the global economy.

DRIVEN ABROAD

The Outsourcing of America

Ron French

RDR Books
Muskegon, Michigan

Driven Abroad

RDR Books
1487 Glen Avenue
Muskegon, Michigan 49441
Phone: 510-595-0595
Fax: 510-228-0300
E-mail: read@rdrbooks.com
Website: www.rdrbooks.com

ISBN 1-57143-122-5
After Jan. 1, 2007: 978-1-57143-122-6

Library of Congress Catalog Card Number 2006902962

Photographs © 2006 by Max Ortiz
Design and production: Richard Harris

Distributed in the United Kingdom and Europe by
Roundhouse Publishing Ltd., Millstone, Limers Lane,
Northam, North Devon EX39 2RG, United Kingdom

Printed in Canada

To Valerie

CONTENTS

INTRODUCTION

I come from a factory family. At one time or another most of my relatives have worked on assembly lines, mixing pancake batter, building school desks, canning soup. My mother earned 85 cents an hour in 1951 manufacturing hand-crank seeders. When she retired from another factory 42 years later, she was making $13 an hour—an amount that, with the frugality learned from growing up during the Depression, let her save for retirement a good portion of her take-home pay.

This was rural Indiana, a place where occupational choices were virtually limited to farming and factories. My grandfather and an uncle built school furniture at a local factory; another uncle worked at a plant manufacturing farm equipment.

I worked in a factory in my hometown of North Manchester, Ind., for two summers when I was a teenager, running a machine that rebound old textbooks so they would survive a few more years in the bottom of school lockers. I worked a graveyard shift, sometimes falling asleep at traffic signals as I raced the sun home.

I could still be there, as some of my friends are. Instead, I became the first member of my family to go to college and, through luck and a fear of manual labor, have managed to spend my entire career in front of one computer or another. Yet the factory has always been as close as the next family reunion.

Perhaps that's why I look at Jorge Ruís Puerto with both sympathy and fear.

Jorge is a devoted family man, a Bible-reading Catholic who visits the sick and needy every Wednesday night. He'd still be selling mangoes from the back of his pickup if the truck hadn't broken down. Unable to afford repairs, Jorge took a job in a factory near his home in San Pedro Sula, Honduras. It is a job that pays him 81 cents an hour, less than my mother earned 54 years ago in the United States. It is too little for the 41-year-old even to buy clean drinking water.

That's why I feel sorry for him.

I fear him because the factory in which he works is owned by a U.S. company.

Defining winners and losers

Jorge does a job that until 2004 was done by an American worker. There are millions like him across Latin America, Asia and Eastern Europe, holding jobs that once belonged to Germans, Japanese, Australians, British and Americans. In the world of globalization, people like Jorge are supposed to be the winners, while we are losers.

But standing in the doorstep of his homemade cinderblock home, Jorge doesn't look victorious. He tries to hide his tears from his children as he talks about life in a foreign-owned factory. Gone are the days when he could treat his children to a pizza once a month. Gone is the money for soap to bathe. He puts his faith in

2

the afterlife he reads about in his tattered Bible, because he's lost all faith in the life he leads here in San Pedro Sula.

I met Jorge in the summer of 2004, when photojournalist Max Ortiz and I traveled more than 20,000 miles following the migration of U.S. factory jobs overseas. We rode with workers in a dusty oven of a bus heading from factories to their homes in Mexican slums. We listened to exhausted Hondurans searching for the strength to punch the time clock the next morning. We sang in a karaoke bar in Wuhu, China, with people who thought the Beatles' biggest hit was "Hey Judy."

I expected to find victims and villains. Instead, I found only victims.

In every country I found remarkable people who reminded me of my own family, people caught in a system not of their making, struggling to gain or hold on to their version of the American Dream.

The American Dream, the idea that through hard work, courage and determination anyone can strike it rich, may have originated on our shores, but it has been our most successful export. Workers around the world not only buy into the concept, they call it by the same name. It's not the Mexican Dream in Juárez or the Honduran Dream in San Pedro Sula—it's the American Dream. Even peasant girls from the rural interior of China describe the American Dream in virtually the same terms as blue-collar workers in Dallas or Chicago.

But an amazing thing happens as you cross borders. Though the definition of the American Dream remains the same, the emotions it evokes change.

In U.S. factories, talk of the American Dream today evokes both reminiscence for the past and cynicism toward the future. In Mexico, the dream sparks envy and anger. In Honduras, the dream conjures naïve gratefulness. In China, it reaffirms seemingly bottomless ambition.

Those divergent feelings are caused by a force few understand: the globalization of jobs.

Outsourcing seems like a much older story in the United States than it actually is. American companies didn't begin shipping jobs overseas in earnest until the 1960s, and it was the 1980s before that trickle of jobs across the border became a tidal wave.

By the turn of the century, outsourcing had become the savior of countless businesses and the scourge of countless working families. Factory owners all knew competitors who had moved overseas and seen profits rise. They also knew competitors who hadn't moved and been driven out of business.

Many blue-collar workers knew someone whose job had been shipped overseas. Many more feared their own jobs were no longer safe.

Dueling mythologies grew, one purveyed by the people cashing paychecks and the other by the people signing those checks. There seemed to be no common ground.

Black, white and lots of gray

Type Amazon.com into your computer. When the Internet bookseller site pops up, type "outsourcing" into the search function. In March 2006, Amazon carried 1,586 entries for books and articles on the subject, many with titles like these:

"The Outsourcing Revolution: Why it Makes Sense and How to do it Right"

"Offshore Outsourcing: Business Models, ROI and Best Practices"

"Outsourcing to India"

"Metrics and Incentives for Outsourcing: Driving Peak Performance"

"Outsourcing Training and Education"

The vast majority of books written on the subject are how-to books for CEOs. Most leave little doubt about the riches that await companies that send jobs overseas.

"Outsourcing has unparalleled power to generate value and wealth for those who learn to apply its principles effectively," promises the product description for "Turning Lead into Gold: The Demystification of Outsourcing."

If a little outsourcing is good for the bottom line, think what a lot of outsourcing could do, says the author of "Outsourcing for Radical Change: A Bold Approach to Enterprise Transformation.

"For years, companies have outsourced service functions like IT and facilities management with an eye toward streamlining overall corporate efficiency," the publisher writes in the book description. "But a new model—transformational outsourcing—can make big changes happen quickly . . . by outsourcing not just support areas but core business functions."

Lost your job to someone making a tenth of your salary in Vietnam? No problem, says the publisher of "The Black Book of Outsourcing: How to Manage Changes, Challenges and Opportunities."

"Those who have lost jobs to outsourcing can land on their feet by taking advantage of new opportunities in the outsourcing industry," the publisher beams in the book description.

Reading these books (or even just the titles and product descriptions) leads you to believe outsourcing is the cure for whatever ails the U.S. economy, that the biggest question about globalization is what to do with all the frequent flier miles you'll earn jetting to your factory in Thailand.

Now turn away from your computer and with your remote control flick to CNN. Lou Dobbs is railing against soulless corporations sucking the lifeblood out of America's middle class. In his regular feature called "Exporting America" and in a book of the same name, Dobbs declares that outsourcing is unpatriotic.

"Never have there been fewer corporate leaders willing to commit to the national interest over self-interest, to the good of their country rather than the company they lead," Dobbs writes.

Dobbs' website lists more than 1,000 U.S. companies "sending American jobs overseas or choosing to employ cheap overseas labor instead of American workers."

Viewers are left with the impression that American businessmen are greedy bastards who would outsource their children to India if that didn't mean driving them to cricket practice.

Beneath the vitriol are people like Jorge and my mother, people for whom outsourcing is more than an academic exercise or political debate. The story of globalization is really the story of millions of people whose lives have been forever changed by forces outside their control, and often beyond their understanding.

I wanted to tell their story and, to the best of my limited ability, stumble toward explaining the economics. The narrative that would tie the loose strings of that story together would be tale of one product, a widget, and its odyssey as its makers searched for cheaper and cheaper labor.

Being a newspaper reporter at *The Detroit News,* it seemed natural to find my widget inside Detroit's auto industry.

Outsourcing checklists

There are thousands of parts in a car, and the likelihood of any one of them being manufactured overseas is determined by several factors:

❏ *Weight and size.* If you produce something overseas, you have to ship it back to America. The heavier the item, the higher the shipping costs. Transmissions, for example are very heavy. While they could be manufactured cheaper overseas, shipping would eliminate the savings. In outsourcing, size matters. You can't fit as many bumpers on a container ship as you can ball bearings.

❏ *Complexity.* The simpler the part, the more likely it will be manufactured overseas. Many employees now working in U.S.-owned factories in Latin American and Asia have never before worked in a factory. Cheap labor isn't cheap if new workers make too many mistakes. Too many "spoils" can even cause companies to lose contracts.

❏ *Labor intensity.* Some parts take a lot of hands to manufacture, while others don't. If one worker can manufacture hundreds of parts by pushing a button on a machine, there is little labor-cost savings moving overseas. In the same way, if a company can eliminate high-paid American workers by automating the workplace, there's little need to move.

American workers who make small, simple products that are resistant to automation are the most likely to lose their jobs. Hundreds of auto parts are manufactured overseas today, but one is the poster child for offshoring: the automotive wire harness. The wire harness is a bundle of cables. It is light and easily packed into boxes for shipment to U.S. assembly plants. It's a simple collection of cables and connections that has remained virtually unchanged in a half-century. Yet production of the wire harness is tough to automate. Some wire harnesses will be touched by more than 20 workers before they are complete, making it one of the most labor-intensive parts in a car. Machines have been built that can do some of the work, but it's cheaper to pay a dozen workers in China 50 cents an hour to build wire harnesses than to invest in those machines.

Because of those factors, wire harness workers in the United States are now as rare as California condors. Almost all automotive wire harnesses are made overseas.

Not surprisingly, the major manufacturers of automotive wire harnesses refused to let us visit their factories in Latin America and Asia. Sending jobs overseas is good business but bad publicity. Companies didn't want their names associated with the business model they embraced.

I called dozens of wire harness manufacturers, and got the same answer or no answer at all. When I was about to give up, Hal Zaima returned my call.

Zaima was owner of Clements Manufacturing, a Michigan manufacturer of wire harnesses. He had moved hundreds of jobs overseas, and was in the process of moving more. He had no choice, he said. It was move or go out of business.

Zaima agreed to let us visit his factories in Michigan, Mexico, Honduras and China. He let us interview workers in each country, and gave us an inside look at the finances that were driving his company and others abroad.

We knew before we left that American jobs were being outsourced. It wasn't until we returned that we understood that jobs were only part of it—our dreams were outsourced, too.

CHAPTER ONE

GLOBALIZED

Huang Wei's future and Deb Coverdill's past are linked by a bundle of color-coded wires.

Both are shy and soft-spoken, with eyes that dart to the floor when a stranger approaches. Both dote on their families. They even work for the same small company.

But there, the similarities end.

In August 2004, Coverdill's factory was for sale and her job in jeopardy. Coverdill had seen hundreds of co-workers laid off and machinery shipped overseas from her automotive wire harness plant in rural Michigan. Generations of her family had earned their livings in factories like the one in which the 46-year-old toiled. Factory jobs had become a kind of blue-collar birthright for millions of Americans—for tens of thousands just in the counties surrounding Detroit's huge auto plants—and Coverdill now saw that birthright slipping away.

As Coverdill punched out for the day in the cool of late afternoon, Huang rode her electric bicycle through the morning heat on the other side of the world. At 22, she was starting a new life far away from the rice fields of her ancestors in a modern factory in Wuhu, China.

For their similar work, Coverdill earned 31 times more money than Huang. Yet Coverdill fretted over her future while Huang bubbled with enthusiasm, unaware that her new job once belonged to a Michigan worker.

Both made wire harnesses, the unheralded bundles of cables that light your car's headlights and power its windows. It's just one part among thousands in a car, which itself is just one of tens of thousands of consumer goods manufactured across the United States. But the migration of wire harness jobs from Michigan to Mexico first and, now, to Central America and Asia, offers a glimpse into the economic forces shaping industry across the globe today.

A global globalization problem

It's not just an American problem. Workers in many industrialized countries also are losing their jobs to foreign factories.

Japanese companies now routinely close plants and move them to nearby China, where labor can be 50 times cheaper.

In the United Kingdom, thousands of jobs have moved to India. Because England currently enjoys low unemployment rates, such outsourcing hasn't caused the public furor it has in the United States. "A lot of call centers have moved to India," said Richard Hollingham, a BBC reporter who has done stories on outsourcing to India. "But the chances are, if there's a call center in London, it's going to be manned by Indians anyway. So what difference does it make if you call and talk to an Indian in the U.K. or an Indian in New Delhi?"

But even in a country so accepting of globalization, there was a public outcry several years ago when Hornby, an iconic British manufacturer of toy trains, moved its factory to China.

Hornby recently purchased several other European toy train manufacturers, with plans to move their production to China, also.

The Czech Republic is known as the "China of Europe," as factories from Western Europe, Korea and Japan move production to the former Communist-bloc country to take advantage of cheaper labor.

Wages for factory workers in the Czech Republic are one-fifth of wages in neighboring Germany, and benefits, such as health care, are lower. "They (the Czech Republic) have attracted so much foreign investment that they've replaced much of local production (lost after the collapse of communism)," said Jan Svegnar, a professor of economics at the University of Michigan and one of the chief architects of Czech economic reform after the fall of Communism. "They have inexpensive labor compared to the education level of workers."

The German auto industry has moved thousands of jobs across the border, causing an outcry from German labor unions. In early 2005, German automaker Volkswagen announced an expansion of a plant in the Czech Republic while shrinking its workforce in Germany.

Siemens VDO has warned its German workforce: work longer hours for the same paycheck or the company will move production to the Czech Republic.

But Czech workers aren't safe, either: Companies are scouring Eastern Europe for even cheaper labor. Some factories have recently moved from the Czech Republic to the Ukraine, where workers will toil for half the pay of Czech workers and one-tenth that of Germans.

Outsourcing arms race

Auto companies seem locked in an arms race to produce more and more of their vehicle parts in low-wage nations. By 2010, Ford expects 50 percent of its car parts will come from overseas—twice its foreign-part ratio in 2005. General Motors and DaimlerChrysler are similarly increasing their overseas production.

Auto suppliers like the company for which Coverdill and Huang work, KenSa LLC, based in Sterling Heights, Michigan, face intense pressure to move manufacturing operations overseas to cut labor costs. General Motors, Ford and Daimler Chrysler, ensnared in their own struggle to survive, bully auto parts companies to move offshore, setting prices for parts that can often only be met by lower wages. Once one parts manufacturer moves, others must follow to match prices. For some companies, offshoring is a choice not between large and moderate profits, but between survival and bankruptcy.

But to workers, the difference between outsourcing and company closures is only a matter of semantics. Either way, they lose their jobs. According to the Economic Policy Institute, the U.S. lost 1.4 million jobs to China between 1989 and 2003, and another 879,000 jobs to Mexico and Canada since the North American Free Trade agreement took effect in 1994.

Michigan, where Coverdill works, has been hit hard by offshoring. The state lost 51,466 jobs to Mexico and Canada between 1994 and 2002 (the third most in the nation), and another 50,000 to China. One study warned that offshoring could cost Michigan another 46,000 jobs between 2005 and 2012—the equivalent of two packed buses of workers rolling across the Ambassador Bridge from Detroit into Canada every week.

That exodus threatens not just jobs, but a way of life. For generations, U.S. laborers parlayed assembly line jobs into the American Dream, supporting middle-class homes and soft retirements on comfortable union salaries. As those jobs are exported to cheaper countries, blue-collar workers are taking jobs for less pay and worse benefits.

Even those who have held on to their jobs have been hurt. The average United Auto Worker has lost five hours of overtime per week since 1997, a loss of about $10,000 per year. The annual cash bonuses paid by Detroit automakers to factory workers also have declined in recent years. At Ford, for example, bonuses averaged $6,700 as recently as 2000. In 2004, the average profit-sharing bonus was $600.

The result: Bankruptcies among UAW workers, among the best-paid blue-collar workers in the United States, are rising 10 percent a year. More than 10,000 UAW members have filed for bankruptcy since 2002.

Just how far the tide had turned became clear in October 2005, when Delphi Corp., the second-largest parts supplier in the United States, declared bankruptcy. The company was expected to emerge from bankruptcy reorganization, but many of its American workers won't.

Delphi had 44 U.S. factories at the time of the bankruptcy, where UAW employees made between $25 and $30 an hour plus good health care and pensions.

The bankruptcy allows Delphi to ask the courts to break its

contracts with the UAW. Once those contracts are broken, Delphi plans to move most of the company's 33,000 U.S. union factory jobs overseas.

Delphi Chairman Robert S. "Steve" Miller, who had already led two huge American companies through bankruptcy, said the decision to move jobs overseas was a question of economics, not morality.

"Philosophers can speculate about fairness," Miller told a press conference shortly after the bankruptcy. "I have to deal with reality."

"Paying $65 an hour (pay and benefits) for someone mowing the lawn at one of our plants is just not going to cut it," Miller said. "People don't want to hear it. But I'm going to do what it takes to lead a restructuring of this company and perhaps this industry."

Delphi was asking the few U.S. workers who kept their jobs to take pay cuts of more than 63 percent—from $26 and hour to $10 an hour.

Meanwhile, Delphi executives were given promises of bigger bonuses if they were laid off in the bankruptcy.

"They (U.S. factory workers) pursued the American Dream and globalization has swept over them," Miller said. "They are extremely angry, and they look at me. I understand it, and I forgive it."

Workers may not be as forgiving.

How do you say "ouch" in Spanish?

The tale of Coverdill and workers like her across the United States are only the best known chapters of a complex and evolving story. Pundits and politicians often portray outsourcing as a zero-sum game, in which every U.S. tear is matched by a Mexican cheer.

But the flood of U.S. jobs into low-wage countries has been

a mixed blessing overseas. Thousands of Mexican workers who took American jobs a decade ago are now losing them to workers in countries offering even cheaper labor. In Honduras, many workers make too little at factories to take their children to Pizza Hut. In China, millions are leaving farms for factories in cities,where they are sparking a new and unpredictable cultural revolution. Now, even in China jobs are moving, as foreign companies race across the vast nation searching for peasants who will work for a few cents less. Chinese factory workers in Shanghai earning about 80 cents an hour are losing jobs to the children of Anhui Province rice farmers willing to toil for half that amount. It is the law of modern global economics: no job is safe as long as someone in the world is willing to do it for less.

Today, the fate of workers in a small Michigan factory is linked to that of workers across the globe in ways unimaginable in the past and uncontrollable in the future. It is a story of economic realities and human drama, where the winners are almost indistinguishable from the losers.

In a come-to-Jesus meeting with auto suppliers in September 2004, Chrysler CEO Dieter Zetsche warned suppliers that they must "adapt or die." And "adapt" means one thing—keep moving.

Is there a limit to this global game of leap frog? How low can wages go? How many more incentives do local communities have to offer too keep jobs for their residents? These questions are being asked by business, labor and government. In the near term, it's likely that Zetsche's maxim is credible and worrisome for everyone in the business world.

Even him.

What KenSa manufactures

Wire harnesses are the nervous system of an auto, connecting virtually every component that moves, squawks or lights.

❶ Controls side lights
❷ Controls turn signals
❸ Controls headlights
❹ Monitors overheating
❺ Makes engine adjust to burn low-grade or bad fuel.
❻ Controls heat

❼ Multi-wire relay box
❽ Controls windshield wipers
❾ Blows heat and air conditioning
❿ Controls air conditioning
⓫ Dims rearview mirror when bright light enters rear windshield
⓬ Controls wiper fluid

⓭ Moves seat for cars with multiple drivers
⓮ Moves steering wheel for cars with multiple drivers
⓯ Multi-wire fuse box
⓰ Controls bass speaker
⓱ Controls lights in door
⓲ Senses if door is ajar
⓳ Locks door
⓴ Senses if seat belt is unfastened
㉑ Adds stability when car skids
㉒ Monitors fuel passing through gas lines
㉓ Monitors fuel pump

Wire harness facts:

■ **Electricity in the wires:** 12 volts, the same as 8 flashlight batteries ■ **Amount of wire in today's cars:** About 200 feet ■ **Number of electrical circuits:** As many as 1,200 ■ **Cost in the purchase price of a car:** $750 to $1,200.

Source: Zukon Co.   *Aaron Hightower / The Detroit News*

CHAPTER TWO

HARBOR BEACH, MICHIGAN

They call themselves the sole survivors with half-hearted laughs that echo through the nearly empty factory in Harbor Beach, Michigan.

There were 350 of them not long ago. But on a drizzly day in early October 2004, the seven workers hunched over picnic tables eating Cheetos and chili represent about half the U.S. assembly line workforce of KenSa LLC, a Michigan wire harness manufacturer. They were afraid and frustrated and angry. None was sure who to blame.

John Hardy has survived round after round of layoffs. He was 42, with a beer belly and a ponytail that flicks across his shoulders when he shakes his head in resignation. Hardy looked out the window of a vacant loading dock at a For Sale sign stuck in the grass. "They're not making enough to pay the electric bill," said Hardy. "Something's gotta happen."

One hundred miles to the south, KenSa owner Hal Zaima emerged from his company headquarters looking grim. A major

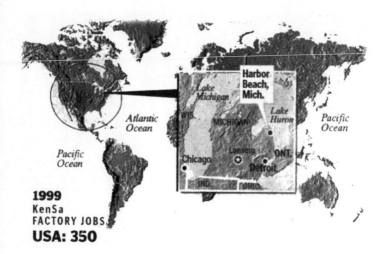

1999
KenSa
FACTORY JOBS.
USA: 350

customer wanted a 25-percent price cut from Zaima's wire harness company. "And they want it back-dated to the beginning of the year," Zaima said, shaking his head. "They want us to write a check for their overpayment." Zaima is a ball of energy, a short Japanese-American seemingly always on the verge of running out of his blue Oxford shirt. The ex-Army Ranger is accustomed to battles, but it's been a long, tough fight for KenSa.

While automakers design and assemble cars and trucks, they rely on suppliers to produce more than half of each vehicle's content. Big suppliers, such as Delphi Corporation, in turn rely on smaller companies to deliver thousands of parts needed to build complete modules, such as instrument panels, that can be plugged into the vehicle. Small auto suppliers buy individual parts from even smaller shops.

This multi-billion dollar supply chain forms the backbone of the auto industry. And as global competition increases, the drive to lower costs seeps down the chain. Every manufacturer in the chain—from

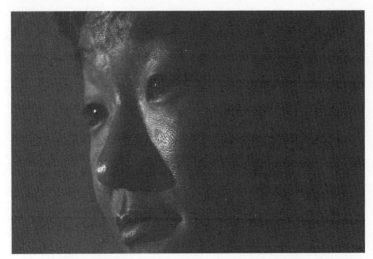

*KenSa owner Hal Zaima says his company would have gone
out of business if it had kept its jobs in the United States.*

major automakers to the mom-and-pop company that makes plastic
radio knobs—is under pressure to reduce prices. For many, the only
option is shifting production to low-wage countries.

Until 2000, KenSa made everything in Michigan. On the verge
of going under, the company moved hundreds of Michigan jobs
to Mexico. When that wasn't enough, it laid off more Michigan
workers and opened a plant in Honduras. In summer 2004, hoping
to save more money, KenSa negotiated to buy controlling interest
in a factory in China.

Each move that helped the company survive made survival
more tenuous for its employees in the United States.

"Everything is being driven by cost," Zaima said. "At the end
of the day, I wonder if we're benefiting."

Between 2000 and 2004, 2.7 million American factory jobs disappeared. Some were eliminated through increased automation, but many others have been lost to cheaper labor in other countries. Michigan, home of America's auto industry, lost 175,000 manufacturing jobs in that time. Auto suppliers alone lost 50,000 jobs.

In just one 12-month period alone, from the third quarter of 2003 to the third quarter of 2004, the motor vehicle and parts industry, which accounts for one third of Michigan manufacturing jobs, suffered 84 percent of manufacturing job losses, according to the U.S. Bureau of Labor Statistics.

Eighteen thousand four hundred people lost their jobs.

In one state.

In one year.

That trend is accelerating. North American auto suppliers will close plants and move as much as 20 percent of their production to lower-cost regions by 2010, according to a survey conducted in 2004 by Roland Berger Strategy Consultants in Troy, Michigan That means 127,000 jobs in American factories like KenSa's Harbor Beach plant will vanish by the end of the decade.

The loss of almost 350 assembly line workers at KenSa is barely a blip on the economic radar—a company that size has in effect closed its doors in Michigan every 12 days since January 2001. Yet KenSa is representative of thousands of small American companies struggling to survive in an increasingly hostile global economy. Its workers' plight is a familiar one, from shuttered textile mills of North Carolina to closed semiconductor plants in California.

Few products have moved more than the wire harness, the low-skill, high-labor car part. KenSa, the new name for the former

A lone worker builds automotive wire harnesses in a near-empty factory in Michigan. By the summer of 2004, most jobs at KenSa had been shipped overseas.

Clements Manufacturing, stuck around longer than most suppliers in the $6 billion wire harness industry. The company survived in Michigan because it paid most of its workers about $7.50 an hour—about a third of the pay members of the United Auto Workers would get for the same job.

Today, even pay hovering close to the U.S. minimum wage is too lavish to maintain contracts with auto companies.

Facing pressure to slash prices another 25 percent, Zaima had to find more cuts. The only thing to do was to look toward Harbor Beach and the sole survivors.

Future of auto supply business lies overseas

Highway 25 skims along the edge of Lake Huron in Michigan's Thumb, past modest homes and sugar beet fields. At dawn, there are often more deer than cars on the road, and John Nye keeps a bleary eye out for the animals as he tries to get a signal on his cell phone.

The KenSa director of operations grew up here, where his friends' parents worked the farms and factories around Ubly, Argyle and Bad Axe. Most of those factories are gone now, including three owned by KenSa. Nye drives an hour each day to reach the company's last plant, the Harbor Beach factory that in October 2004 was virtually an empty shell.

Nye is a popular boss among the remaining workers, yet he bluntly acknowledges that Harbor Beach represents the past; the future is overseas.

"For a company our size to be where we're at (in the world) is pretty cool," Nye said. "It's a global thing."

Nye is a wire harness pro. He can pick up a tangle of wires and identify it as a trailer harness for a 2000 Chrysler Prowler or an ignition harness for a '69 Road Runner. He knows there are 1,200 electronic circuits in a new Lincoln Town Car and, if forced to, he could name most of them.

Nye began working in the wire harness business in 1971, at the end of the golden era of the American auto industry. Auto parts workers like those in Harbor Beach were paid good money. The Big Three bought their auto parts and built cars with their own well-paid workers. Workers up and down the food chain bought the cars.

It was a fragile economic ecosystem, with everyone dependent upon and benefiting from each other.

In the late 1970s, cracks appeared in the system.

First, Americans started buying Japanese cars, eating into the Big Three's market share. Next Nissan, Toyota and Honda opened assembly plants in North America to meet the growing demand.

The Japanese cars were more fuel-efficient and reliable, but they had another, less noticeable advantage over their American counterparts.

Decades of successful bargaining by the UAW obtained generous health care and pension benefits for its members. The Japanese have younger workforces at their U.S. factories—they've been hiring only since the mid-1980s and have few retirees. By contrast, GM has 2.5 retirees for every active worker in North America.

Today, the price tag on every new General Motors car and truck includes $1,824 just to pay for pension and health care benefits for retired GM employees and their spouses, according to Morgan Stanley. To put that in perspective, buyers of a new Cadillac Escalade or Chevy Impala are paying twice as much for GM retiree benefits than they are for all the wiring in those vehicles.

By comparison, Toyota's cost for retiree benefits is $186 per vehicle—one-tenth that of GM. Before vehicles roll off the assembly line, Toyota already has a $1,638 advantage on GM.

The massive retiree obligations increased pressure on the Big Three to drive down costs. The automakers began demanding deep price concessions from parts suppliers.

Those cuts rippled down from major component manufacturers such as Lear Corporation and Delphi Corporation, to smaller parts makers scattered across the country.

Desperate companies scoured budgets for savings. The costs of material and utilities were rising. But there were people willing to work for less money just across the border in Mexico.

In a sense, American autoworkers are losing jobs today because of their earlier victories at the negotiating table, said Kim Hill of the Center for Automotive Research, an auto industry think tank based in Ann Arbor.

"It's a damn shame," Hill said. "It used to be almost a social contract. People signed up for these jobs and they're just working along, and the (global economy) comes along and kicks them in the butt."

Small-town loyalty vs. big-time profits

Clements Manufacturing, the predecessor of KenSa, was founded 58 years ago as a manufacturer of wire picture frame hangers. It branched into electronic wiring in the 1950s and into automotive wiring in the 1960s.

At one time, Clements had six plants in Michigan, small operations in small towns supplying parts to nearby auto assembly plants.

Kathy Goheen began working at Clements in 1955 and owned the company through the 1980s and 1990s. She watched as the wire harness plants that dotted the region disappeared. Some locked their doors and moved to Mexico. Others, out of stubbornness or loyalty to their workers, refused to leave America and eventually went bankrupt.

"Many times we were told, 'You have to go offshore or you're not going to get our business.' But somehow, some way, we held on."

The public and politicians complained about sending jobs overseas, but Wall Street had a different response. When publicly traded auto suppliers announced plans to move jobs overseas, their stock typically rose, said Kevin Tynan, an auto industry stock analyst for Argus Research.

Even more than their European and Japanese rivals, U.S. companies were under pressure to report short-term profit growth and boost stock prices.

"An economist could look at it as a negative for our economy," Tynan said, "but an analyst would look at it as a positive for reducing fixed costs."

Publicly traded companies had to answer to their stockholders and boards of directors, but Kathy Goheen answered to the clerk at Venckier Foods and the waitress at Blower's Café in her small hometown. She grew up with her workers and she said in 2004 that while she was owner, she wasn't going to abandon them, even if it cost her money.

"I had a lot of loyalties to these small towns," Goheen said. "There were an awful lot of people who didn't have the capability to do a lot of other things. They were good, hardworking people."

As recently as the late 1990s, Clements factories were packed with workers hustling pallet after pallet of wire harnesses to assembly plants across the Midwest. Employees often worked 50 to 60 hours a week to keep up with orders.

Since selling her company in 1998 to Hal Zaima, Goheen has watched in dismay as one after another of her factories has shut down. By January 2004, the company's U.S. payroll had dwindled to 40 administrative staff in Sterling Heights and 80 factory workers in Harbor Beach.

Zaima has a different recollection of that period. He says Goheen's children were actively involved in moving jobs to Mexico. Loyalty to small-town workers ended when the Goheen family had a chance to make millions selling the company.

"It's heartbreaking," Goheen said. "The world has become a totally different place."

Conflict and ambition in Coach Class

Hal Zaima can compare and contrast cell phone reception in provincial China with that in Michigan's Thumb. He e-mails employees in Honduras while watching his 12-year-old son Lucas play goalie in a Birmingham youth hockey league. He is the personification of Goheen's fears, a globe-hopping entrepreneur owing allegiance to business models rather than communities.

Zaima sees himself less as executioner than messenger of that new economic reality. In today's auto industry, he knows employees are commodities to be shuffled around the globe like the parts they produce. He is conflicted about the moves he makes, but he also feels powerless to stop them. KenSa can either ride the waves or sink beneath them.

It's been a long trip from the sugar cane fields of Hawaii, where his grandfather, a Japanese immigrant, labored during the Depression. His father fought in Europe in World War II and afterward helped rebuild war-torn Japan.

Zaima was born in Japan, where he attended American military schools. He followed his father into the service, first attending West Point then joining the Rangers, an elite Army unit. While in the Rangers, Zaima earned a master's degree in business administration by attending night school.

He helped a Japanese auto parts company set up joint ventures in the United States, Europe and Australia, living on airplane food and catnaps.

Zaima wanted his own business. The risks were greater, but so were the rewards. He saw in Clements a company that was ripe for expansion. He bought 51 percent of the company in 1998 and the rest in 2002. As sole owner, Zaima is able to respond quickly to the changing business climate. He wasted no time, moving half his company's jobs to Mexico within 18 months of taking over.

It is still a small company by Detroit standards, perhaps the eighth- or ninth-largest wire harness manufacture in the U.S. It provides 4 percent of the battery cables and less than 1 percent of the wire harnesses for U.S. assembly plants, but Zaima has big plans. He wants to increase global sales from $40 million to $500 million in 10 years. The sales will be primarily to U.S. companies, but the manufacture will be strictly offshore.

Even the new name of the company—KenSa, a combination of the names of his father Kenneth and mother Satsuki—was a bow to offshoring. "The old name was Clements Manufacturing of Michigan LLC," Zaima said. "KenSa is much easier to pronounce around the world."

A lifestyle into limbo

About 70 workers gathered around Zaima in the Harbor Beach factory cafeteria in January 2004.

Things weren't going well, Zaima told them. He was trying to sell the plant.

If he couldn't find a buyer, the factory would close.

"Here we go again," Hardy thought after the meeting. He had already worked at two auto industry plants that went belly-up, and this looked like the third.

For years, Hardy had slid down the economic ladder. By 2004, he was earning less than half of what he made just a few years earlier and felt lucky to bring home any paycheck at all.

Hardy lived in what outsiders call the heartland, a hodgepodge of small towns and farms far away from the bustling cities and suburbs. It is in these small towns where outsourcing has hit like a sledgehammer.

When a factory closes in suburban Detroit, workers have dozens if not hundreds of other factories within a reasonable commute to which they can apply for work. But in Harbor Beach, with a population under 2,000 and only a handful of employers, the closure of one factory can be devastating.

"They're losing jobs in Harbor Beach. They're losing jobs in Bad Axe. Jobs in Sebewaing seem shaky," said Pam Semp, owner of The Corner Store in Harbor Beach. "It affects everything."

Empty storefronts dot picturesque downtowns. School enrollment is dropping. Salaries of the jobs that remain are held down by the number of people desperate for work, any work.

Hardy didn't give a damn about the macroeconomics of outsourcing, but he cared deeply about his town, his friends and his family, and they were all getting screwed.

28

"It's like the waves are all going the wrong way," Hardy said.

"I don't think the tide's coming back."

Throughout 2004, layoffs continued at the plant. By October of that year, the number of assembly workers had dwindled to 15, all clinging to a fading way of life. Zaima kept the doors open on wire harness orders too small for the big factories to bother with. There were orders for specialty harnesses such as trailer hitches and replacement parts for aging American cars. But even those scraps were getting rare.

"Do we still have work? We wonder day to day," said Doug Ross, 42, of Deckerville. "We're all thinking that (our jobs) are going to be here. We can't look at it any other way."

Boxes of machinery being shipped from a Michigan factory to Honduras is a cruel reminder that jobs are moving to developing countries.

A large section of the plant was bare, with lights turned out. Other areas had one or two employees working among a dozen workstations.

On an October afternoon, Todd Klaus painstakingly counted 1,000 tiny plastic parts that were needed at a new bustling plant operated by the company in Honduras. The 37-year-old Deckerville man counted them slowly so he didn't run out of work.

Hardy disassembled metal equipment stands and shipped them to another of the company's factories, this one in Mexico.

"People give me a hard time," Hardy said. "They say I'm packing up their jobs. But if I didn't do it, someone else would."

Deb Coverdill took the same attitude when she helped train Mexican workers to do the jobs of Americans in 2000. In the spring of 2004, she did the same in Honduras, in effect digging the grave for herself and her coworkers. She'd looked the devil in the eyes and come back with something her buddies in Harbor Beach couldn't grasp: Empathy for those on the other end of the wire harness. The people in Mexico and Honduras were just like her Harbor Beach friends, only a hell of a lot poorer.

"They're taking our jobs, but they're trying to improve their lives over there," said Coverdill, 46, of Deckerville. "It's such a poor country. You can't blame them.

"They're just part of the whole scenario—they're benefiting and we're losing."

PROFILE: JOHN HARDY

One of the company's holdouts adjusts to
a life without certainty

John Hardy has learned to adjust to the new economics of the auto industry.

He drinks less beer. He smokes generic cigarettes. If something breaks in the house, he waits longer to get it fixed.

In a larger sense, he guesses that's what his employer is doing.

"You can't blame the owners," said Hardy, 42. "It's got to be the Big Three themselves. They keep cutting our prices on what they want to pay. If you keep cutting, something's got to give."

Hardy makes about $25,000 a year as the sole maintenance worker at KenSa's factory in Harbor Beach. It's not enough to make him rich, but in Michigan's rural thumb, it's enough for a pretty good life.

Hardy lives in a three-bedroom ranch home with his wife and one stepchild on a one-acre lot filled with pine trees. He refurbishes old Honda dirt bikes in a garage that is an American guy's dream: There's a television, VCR, refrigerator, and a karaoke machine sitting next to power tools.

He spends a lot of time out there, tinkering with engines and thinking. Hardy has already worked at two auto industry factories that closed. He made close to $60,000 a year at a shop that assembled limousines. When it closed, he took a job at the KenSa plant in Deckerville. It closed about two years ago, and he transferred to the Harbor Beach plant.

He's seeing the same signs of trouble again.

"I've seen it before," Hardy said. "We used to have skids of wire harnesses going out every day. Now, it's one skid every couple days." Since January, he's gone to work each day, not knowing if it would be his last.

"My wife worked at Aunt Jane's Pickles for 20 years before it closed," Hardy said. "They say no one is going to have the same job forever like they used to.

"What's going to happen in this area in five years? There are some really talented people around here," Hardy said. "Industry is just fading away."

At the limousine factory, Hardy was laid off without notice one day. "This has dragged on for years," he said. It's like the difference between a heart attack and cancer. "Either one will kill you, but one gives you too much time to think about it."

Hardy lights a cigarette. "When does it end? Before you know it, I'm going to be the one living in a dirt-floor shack in Honduras."

John Hardy has worked at two auto parts companies
that closed by 2004, and his third was in danger of closing.

CHAPTER THREE

LIFE AFTER LAYOFF

Just how much the workers in Harbor Beach stood to lose could be seen 150 miles to the south at another shell of a factory where production moved out of the United States. In 2001, Lear Seating Plant 2 in Romulus, Michigan, shut down and moved across the Detroit River to Canada. Two years later I talked to more than 100 of those workers to see how they'd fared.

Many remained unemployed 24 months after losing their jobs, and almost all earned less than they did at Lear. Less than half found other factory work. Others are now police officers, surgical technicians and chefs. But even the success stories are footnoted with lost homes, lost marriages and lost hopes.

After past economic downturns, factory jobs returned. This time, they won't. Economists say the American economy and its workers can't count on an economic rebound, a strengthening economy or an upsurge in the auto market.

Former factory workers like Scott Caldwell have discovered that reinventing themselves is a tiring and expensive process.

At 36, he was at least a decade older than his fellow student nurses at Oakwood Hospital in Dearborn, Michigan. Unlike his new coworkers, his resume reflected more grit than grades. He'd built boat trailers and car seats along Metro Detroit's assembly lines, earning good pay while keeping the region's economy buzzing one bolt at a time.

The hire date Caldwell scribbled on his hospital employment form—December 29, 2003—was more than two years after he and 327 others lost their jobs at Lear Seating. For 27 months, the Taylor resident scraped by on unemployment benefits while attending school, awaiting the day he could put his pink slip behind him.

"Three years ago, I thought I'd put in my 30 years at Lear and retire," Caldwell said. "Now, I just want a job I know will be there in 30 years."

The plant closing barely made the newspapers. But the choices made by the former workers of this shuttered auto supplier reflect the pitfalls and hopes of thousands like them, as well as a national economy facing the same tough choices.

Go home. The plant is closed.

Managers herded the day shift workers into the cafeteria of Lear-Seating Plant Two in Romulus for a meeting the morning of October 12, 2001. We'll pay you for today's shift, managers said. Go home. The plant is closed.

Seating plants are the canaries of the auto industry, suffering layoffs and closings at the whiff of an economic downturn. Because of their bulk, and because they are built on a just-in-time schedule, seats must be built close to the assembly plants where they will be bolted into cars. Rom Two, as workers called the Lear plant, made seats for the Mercury Cougar and Ford Windstar.

Employees often worked 60 hours a week to keep up with demand. But in 2001, the factory became a victim of changing consumer tastes and terrorism.

The Cougar was being discontinued because of poor sales. The Windstar line was moving to a factory in Windsor, Ontario, near the assembly plant where these vans were assembled. For years, the seats were shuttled across the Ambassador Bridge. Added security after September 11 made just-in-time delivery across the international border difficult.

Management notified workers months earlier that the plant was likely to close. That only added fuel to the rumors swirling around the factory floor. One day, workers would talk excitedly of a contract for truck seats that would save their jobs; the next, they'd be certain they were receiving their last paycheck. The morning it became official, Charlene Van Meer recalls a numb acceptance among her co-workers, as if a family member had passed away after a long illness.

Van Meer had a sister, an uncle and a cousin at Ford. Her husband, Tom Van Meer, also a Lear employee, had a father and an uncle at General Motors. Many at Lear were second- and thirdgeneration auto workers accustomed to riding out the ups and downs of the industry. But that day, Charlene Van Meer saw something in her co-workers' eyes she'd never seen:

Fear.

Scott Caldwell walked out of Lear after the meeting not knowing when or where he'd work again. "I have no skills. Anybody can push a screw into a metal seat," Caldwell said. "My God, what do I do now?"

Losing more than a job

In some ways, the workers of Rom Two were luckier than their counterparts at KenSa in Harbor Beach. They knew months in advance that their plant was likely to close. Because production of Windstar seats moved to Canada, the workers qualified for generous retraining benefits through the North American Free Trade Agreement. And in the two years after the closing, Lear offered the vast majority of them temporary or full-time jobs at other Lear plants.

Yet 27 months after most workers lost their jobs (about 60 worked until August 2002), many continue to suffer financially.

Most of the 328 employees of Rom Two made $17.61 an hour plus generous overtime in the fall of 2001. Today, those who have returned to Lear full-time earn more than they did; those who haven't, make less.

Of the 328 employees, 104 work at an adjacent Lear factory making automobile seats, earning about $19 an hour, according to Lear.

A vast majority—90 percent—of 140 former Rom Two workers who did not return to Lear earn less money than they did in 2001.

About 44 percent remained jobless in 2004—more than six times the state jobless rate.

"You can't help but empathize with them," said Chuck Batt, trade program coordinator at the Downriver Community Conference, a Southgate, Michigan organization that coordinated retraining benefits for Rom Two workers. "They're re-entering the workforce at the bottom. These are long-term employees. It's a gut-wrenching experience."

More than 60 Rom Two workers completed training programs

or college degrees. Most believe it will pay off someday. But for many, that day has not yet arrived.

Evelyn Santos attended college full-time for two years after her layoff, earning an associates' degree in December 2003. But days after her graduation, Santos called Lear asking to return to the factory.

"I was done with the factory," said Santos, 31. "But times are hard. You take what you can get."

It wasn't the career path the Detroit resident envisioned when Rom 2 closed.

Moving in with her parents, Santos studied in the small room she shared with her two children. On a typical night, she'd try to make sense of algebra at a desk while her 10-year-old worked on spelling on the floor and her 8-year-old studied his own math assignment.

Times were tough, but she believed they were temporary. "I felt factory jobs were for people who didn't want to go to school," Santos said.

Lear called to offer her a job in 2002, but Santos turned it down. She was enrolled in computer and speech classes at Henry Ford Community College, taking what she believed would be the first steps toward a new career.

Her education has yet to pay off. She sends out resumes and scours the Internet daily, with no luck. "An associate's degree isn't good enough," she said. "I need a bachelor's (degree)."

But her two years of free schooling ended in late 2003. She needed a job.

Lear told Santos to drop off a resume along with a letter explaining why she'd turned down the earlier job offer.

"My parents say, 'Why go back into the factory if that's why you went to school?' But when times are hard, you need to get paid to get insurance for your kids."

Permanent changes in the workforce

The experience of Santos and her fellow Lear workers is typical of those who have lost jobs overseas. When their jobs are outsourced, American factory workers earn an average of 23 percent less in their next position, according to statistics compiled by the AFL-CIO. The vast majority of the manufacturing jobs lost nationwide since 2001 resulted from permanent changes in the economy and will have to be replaced with non-manufacturing work, according to a Federal Reserve Bank of New York study.

Sam D. Kahn, chief economist for the Federal Reserve in Detroit, said Americans should take a longer view of today's economic troubles. "If we look at history, we shouldn't be too despondent over this," Kahn said. "One hundred years ago, one of every two people worked in agriculture. Now it's 2 percent of our population. Nobody is groaning and moaning over this."

The economy, and displaced workers, adjusted.

"Certain jobs we lose because the world is in a competitive situation," Kahn said. "Can we replace those jobs with something better or different? That's the challenge."

It's a challenge that is painful for the affected workers. Economists have the luxury of historical perspective; today's displaced workers are more concerned with paying the mortgage and finding health insurance for their children.

Gail Martinez made $17 an hour at Lear Seating before being laid off in 2001. Two years later, the 45-year-old struggled to support herself and two teen-age sons with a part-time job at McDonald's that paid $8.50 an hour.

"People tell you how devastating it is to lose your job, but you don't realize it until it happens to you," said Martinez. "There's nothing out there that pays anything. You lose money and self-esteem."

Marc Strong lost even more.

Strong kept the arithmetic of his new life in neat, manila folders.

There was the house file, with mortgage and second mortgage balances totaling $120,000, more than the small Lincoln Park home with peeling paint and a furnace on the fritz was worth.

There was the credit card file: $24,000 on various cards; two cars, total owed $18,000; wife Angela's student loans, totaling $50,000.

The couple filed for bankruptcy in 2004, about the same time that the bank foreclosed on their home.

"We're short $1,500 a month on bills," Strong said. "We thought I'd get a decent job. Then, unemployment ran out."

Strong is a big man, 29 years old with a crew cut and a Detroit Pistons jersey. He proudly calls himself a "third-generation factory rat" who grew up to the rhythm of Detroit's assembly lines. Attending the North American International Auto Show in past years, he'd raise a beefy arm above the crowd and point to a leather bucket seat in a Ford Mustang.

"I'd say, 'I may have built that seat.' "

After the plant closed, Strong went to school for a year to become a massage therapist, only to discover "nobody wants a massage from a big guy with kids." He delivered pizzas, built automobile clutches at an Auburn Hills factory for $9.50 an hour and refilled ATMs for $9.25 an hour. Strong spends his days searching for his personal holy grail: a union-pay auto assembly job.

He's filled out so many applications and taken so many drug screens that his left arm remains tender from needle pricks.

"I know the economy is in the dumps and it's cheaper to make it someplace else," Strong said. "But I deserve my chance for the American Dream."

Strong still believes in the dream of his parents and grandparents, the dream of talking sports with the guys on the line while Cougar seats roll past forever; pocket money for pizza and movies; maybe someday a cabin up north. It was the promise of Detroit's blue-collar middle class, nurtured in break rooms from River Rouge to Warren.

In early 2004, he found a job in Warren making truck seats for Ford. The pay: $10.50 an hour.

"This country was built on hard work," he said. "Maybe I am a dinosaur. But the world needs ditch diggers, too. Here I am now, wishing I was back in the factory."

Return to the assembly line or start anew?

It was a $100,000 question: Did Tom and Charlene Van Meer want jobs back at Lear?

The Michigan couple struggled financially after Rom Two closed. Tom Van Meer took a job laying tile, but they were still going into the red by almost $2,000 a month. "We just couldn't pay our bills," Tom said. "She cashed in stock, and I took out a 401(k) loan."

Both received calls offering jobs at Rom One. They'd be doing the same work they performed at Rom Two for similar pay. With one call, one syllable shouted into the phone, their income could go from zero to $100,000.

But saying yes wasn't easy. An auto job was a love affair they sensed would end badly. The seduction of money was tempered by the fear of being jilted in the cafeteria once again. Tom, 30, wanted to go back. "There's a comfort factor there," he said. "I know how to build seats."

He knew he could lose his job again. But how could he justify turning down that kind of money? Maybe the job would last this time. Maybe they'd just had bad luck before and now it was their turn to be lucky. Besides, what would his kids think if he turned away from a job that could mean a Jet Ski, Pistons tickets, even an iPod Mini.

But Charlene felt lucky to be away from Lear. The pneumatic drills made her hands ache so much that she had trouble opening a jar of peanut butter for her children. The fabric she stretched across the seats dried out her hands to the point that she had to soak them in ice water every week. Unlike her husband, the 39-year-old ex Lear employee was building a career as a massage therapist. But the pay, about $300 every two weeks, is what she could earn weekly in overtime alone at Lear.

In the end the couple split the difference. Tom would go back to Lear and Charlene would keep her part-time job as a massage therapist. It was a decision that cost the family about $40,000 a year.

"Christmas would have been better," Tom said.

"You'd have your new truck by now," Charlene said.

"We'd have something in savings," Tom said.

The couple was silent for a long moment.

"We could be better off financially, but in the long run, this is for the best," Tom said. "Who's to say, five years from now, I could get laid off again."

There are days when the hum of the factory calls to Scott Caldwell, days when he's studying physiology alone while his old buddies play poker; days when he curses his rotten credit rating and his bankruptcy.

How easy it would be to drive bolts into metal all day, collect a fat paycheck and go home, like his father did before him, like most of his friends do today.

"There were a lot of days when I wasn't real sure I'd make it," Caldwell said. "It's hard to start over. I'm 36 years old. I've been working for 18 years."

After leaving Lear, the ex-Marine researched careers on the Internet.

"Right now, there's such a huge shortage of nurses, I don't think I could have picked a better field to go into," Caldwell said.

Many didn't have the choice. Some felt they were too old to start a new career. Others were the sole breadwinners in their homes and, unable to survive on about $300 a week they received on unemployment, took whatever work they could find.

"Luckily, I had a wife who was working (as an AAA customer service representative)," Caldwell said.

Soon after the plant closed, the couple sat with a calculator at the kitchen table, figuring their income and expenses. If Scott went to school, it would be tight, but they believed they could make it.

They were wrong. Bills piled up. They took punishing cash advances on their credit cards to pay the mortgage.

The couple declared bankruptcy in 2004.

"Right now, we can't finance an orange," Caldwell said.

He began a job as a student nurse at Oakwood Hospital in Dearborn in early 2004. He made $15 an hour, enough to pay bills until he became a registered nurse the following year. It seemed far off, but looking down the corridor of the cardiac care unit, the factory seemed even farther away.

"It's not the same here," he said. "It feels like . . . I'm accomplishing something."

In early 2004 many Rom Two refugees heard talk that Lear was preparing to open another line at Rom One. Others who had been rehired were troubled by rumors that their new jobs would not last.

Andrea Puchalsky, communications director at Lear felt like she was standing next to a water cooler all day long, being pummeled with the latest intelligence reports. Voice mail stacked up all day long from callers who wanted to know if they would get new jobs, keep their old jobs or if there were someone, anyone at Lear who could share their crystal ball.

Little did they know that more than a thousand miles to the south, workers in a Mexican factory were asking the same questions.

CHAPTER FOUR

JUÁREZ, MEXICO

Rush hour in Juárez begins at 5 a.m. with a convoy of pale buses belching and creaking down the Ejercito Nacional, their white paint barely covering the names of the U.S. schools that discarded them.

In a city of 1.5 million, there are no buses to take children to school, but thousands of buses to take their parents to work. They crisscross the slums, delivering workers to factories. The buses stream by the Guadalupe Cathedral for nearly an hour, the names propped in windshields reading like the U.S. stock exchange: Lear, Jemco, Consico, RCA, Mercury.

Leonardo Acosta rides a bus headed for KenSa, one of the factories that make this the wire harness capital of the world. Acosta works in a clean, bright plant with lively music playing over loud-speakers. A free breakfast buffet includes omelettes cooked to order. Later, the free lunch buffet will feature beef and chicken entrees, soup, rice and beans, salad, dessert, soda and a sandwich bar.

But there's no such thing as a free lunch, even in Mexico.

Mexican factory workers, while far from living the middle

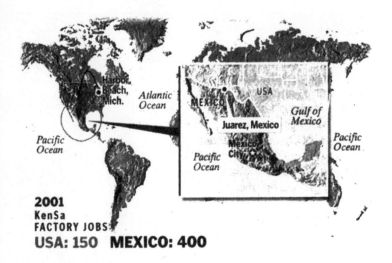

2001
KenSa
FACTORY JOBS
USA: 150 MEXICO: 400

class life of their American counterparts, are being priced out of the market. In Honduras, workers earn half the pay of Mexicans; Chinese workers earn even less.

Mexican workers are in the untenable position of not earning enough for a good life, but too much for job security. It's a treadmill trapping workers in developing countries as they struggle to keep what had been American jobs.

In a dozen years, Mexico has experienced the boom-and-bust cycle that occurred in the United States over decades.

The controversial 1994 North America Free Trade agreement, which removed trade barriers in the region, was expected to foster sustained economic growth in Mexico and raise wages. But Mexico's proximity to the United States has lost cachet as trade barriers have fallen around the world. Once China joined the World Trade Organization in 2001, it became easy to import Chinese auto parts and other goods into North America.

*Buses transport workers from their slum homes
to clean, bright factories each day in Juárez.*

Factories that sprang up virtually overnight have closed or laid off workers almost as quickly, leaving thousands of unemployed Mexicans with little money or hope.

In the front offices of Mexican factories like KenSa, frustration and anxiety abound. Executives look at the numbers on their spreadsheets and see that the same factors that drove jobs from the United States to Mexico are now driving jobs elsewhere.

"Jobs are going," said Charlie Hill, Juárez plant manager for KenSa. "It's going to keep happening as long as customers force the suppliers to cut costs."

KenSa once employed 570 workers here. By 2003, 70 percent of those workers were gone.

Almost half of the factory is empty or used for storage. Some equipment has been shipped to a newer KenSa factory in Honduras. And while the work force at the plant has recently rebounded to about 230, workers and managers alike are learning the dark side of globalization.

"I worry," Acosta said through a translator. "I worry because I need this job."

Few in the U.S. feel sympathy for the plight of Mexico and its workers. They took American jobs, the feeling goes. They're getting their just desserts.

But nothing feels just in Juárez. Unemployed workers face long odds of finding jobs, or even finding enough money to go back to their homes hundreds of miles away.

American Dream, Mexican-style

The river that separates the United States and Mexico goes by different names on each bank. In El Paso it's the Rio Grande, meaning large river; in Juárez it's Río Bravo, or valiant river. Neither name fits the ankle-deep thread of brown water that trickles through this stretch of the border.

From the fetid slum of Anapra, where thousands live in tar paper-and-cardboard huts, labor lawyer Susana Terrazas can look across the river to Coronado, one of El Paso's wealthiest neighborhoods. Anapra residents can hike across the mud flats of the Rio Grande and, if they're not caught by immigration patrols, climb the mountainside to work as maids and gardeners in the $500,000 homes.

"The American Dream is a popular expression in Mexico," said Terrazas. "If you go to that mountain, you can see that life is different, but you can't get it."

Terrazas is a legal bulldog in high heels and a pastel business suit. Years of fighting for the rights of Mexican factory workers have left her cursing and smoking with equal vigor.

"George Bush says come get the American Dream," Terrazas scowled. She waved a cigarette across an expanse of squatters' shacks. "There is no dream here."

In what passes for a blue-collar neighborhood in Juárez, there are no streetlights, no running water and no schools. A row of pink crosses stands in a rutted field that is a favorite dumping ground for the bodies of young women—more than 400 have been mysteriously murdered in Juárez in the past 10 years.

It is a wretched place, made all the more sobering by the fact that most of the adults who live here have full-time jobs. Thousands of workers in Mexico's maquiladoras—the foreign-owned factories along Mexico's border—live in the squalid shacks of Anapra. Their struggles in Juárez have become a symbol of the limits to which U.S. companies have benefited their Mexican workers.

Andres Lugardo brought his family from Acupulco to Juárez looking for a better life. He builds computers for Tatung, a Korean company, earning 350 pesos (about $30) per week, low even by maquiladora standards.

The money is enough for food and little else. The family has meat one day a week, and soup, beans and potatoes the rest of the week.

Lugardo paid $400, the equivalent of more than a year's salary, to take over a squatter's shack in Anapra. The walls are discarded wood pallets. The roof is tar paper held down by rocks.

Like all homes in Anapra, electricity is stolen from power lines. Thick orange extension cords snake across the mud and refuse between shacks. Like seemingly every home in even the worst slums, a television runs around the clock, providing both a dis-

49

traction from the surroundings and a reminder of what life is like outside of Juárez.

"When you have children, you turn the TV on and it says 'Come to Burger King,' but if they take the family, they will spend the whole week's salary," Terrazas said.

Workers often make a tenth of what they would earn across the river in El Paso, while paying American prices for consumer goods. A Whopper, french fries and soft drink at a Juárez Burger King costs 55 pesos, or almost $5. A new pair of Wrangler jeans costs 180 pesos, about $15.

"They say the factories helped Mexico, but it is a lie," Terrazas said. "They send buses to the interior (of Mexico) and tell people 'Come to Juárez, we have good pay, live the American Dream.' When they come here and see the reality, there is no bus to take them back home."

But there are plenty of buses to take them to work.

From boom to bust in a decade

The wire harness is an automotive anachronism, virtually unchanged in design or manufacture since the Depression. Color-coded wires are cut and capped with connectors. The wires are then propped on pegs on vertical boards the size of dining room tables. Maps on the boards tell workers where to wrap electrical tape, where to add connectors, and which wires to pull to the side.

While the rest of the auto industry is highly automated, wire harness factories still depend on hundreds of nimble-fingered workers building one harness at a time. A full-body harness can run the length of a car and be touched by 50 pairs of hands.

Thus, cheap labor can make a big difference for wire harness manufacturers. That's why wire harness factories were among the

María González Huerta works on an assenbly line in Juárez, Mexico.
Many employees in Juárez earn ten times less than
people doing similar work across the river in El Paso.

first to come to Juárez, taking advantage of a special commercial zone allowing U.S. companies to import raw goods to Mexican factories and export finished goods back to the U.S. without being taxed. Today, there are more than 3,000 maquiladoras—a Spanish word meaning to process for free—in Mexico.

By the time KenSa opened its Juárez plant in 2000, there was a fierce labor shortage. The company had a turnover rate of 12 percent per month—in effect hiring and training a complete new workforce every eight months.

A worker could quit his job at 8 a.m. and have a new job across the street at noon," said Rudy Robles, controller at the KenSa Juárez plant.

To attract workers, KenSa and other companies offered subsidized bus transportation to and from employees' homes. When that didn't work, they made the bus rides free. Factories offered free breakfasts and lunches.

Soon, KenSa was offering bonuses for coming to work, and more bonuses for coming to work on time. Employees with good attendance and punctuality could increase their pay by 81 percent. Companies pay 100 percent of health insurance for minimum wage employees, and most of it for those making more.

"There's a misconception about pay," with Americans thinking wages are unconscionably low in Mexico, said Robles. "With the other compensation, it's very attractive."

Terrazas scoffs at the notion that take-home pay of between $50 and $60 a week is attractive.

"If it's so good, why are they living like this?" she asked.

Perpetuating poverty

NAFTA and the new foreign-owned factories have failed to narrow the chasm dividing Mexico's rich and poor. In the past decade in Mexico, the number of billionaires has multiplied, while the incomes of working people have fallen.

"The maquiladoras are an industrial success and a social failure," said Harley Shaiken, a professor specializing in labor in the global economy at the University of California at Berkeley. "Productivity and quality have gone up, but real wages have declined."

A study conducted by the economics department of the National Autonomous University in Mexico City found that Mexican wages have lost 80 percent of their buying power in 20 years. In 1985, minimum wage in a maquiladora could pay for 93.5 percent of a family's basic necessities such as food and lodging; today, it buys 19.3 percent.

As an example, it takes a maquiladora worker in Juárez about an hour to earn enough to buy a kilo (2.2 pounds) of rice, according to a study by the Center for Reflection, Education and Action. By comparison, an American worker unloading that rice at a California shipyard could buy a kilo of rice in three minutes; even an undocumented worker at minimum wage has to work only 12 minutes for the rice.

Foreign-owned factories in developing countries have spawned a new economic term: high-productivity poverty.

Changes in labor laws meant to assist factories have decimated Mexico's once-thriving labor unions. While three-quarters of the workforce in Mexico belonged to unions three decades ago, less than 30 percent do today. The Mexican government follows a policy of suppressing wages in order to attract foreign investment.

"Desperate poverty is nothing new," Shaiken said. "You can see worse poverty in Haiti. But what is unique in Juárez is the contrast between work life and home life.

"These workers are working in the 21st century and living in the 17th century," Shaiken said. "They are dealing with microns and state-of-the-art circuit boards at work, and dealing with medieval diseases like cholera at home."

Yet Mexico dares not raise its minimum wage or increase taxes on the foreign-owned factories, because the nation is already losing jobs to countries where people are willing to work for less. In fact, Mexico President Vincente Fox talks about lowering wages.

In many ways, Mexico was the lab rat for globalization. Over

20 years, multinational corporations, as well as small U.S. companies like KenSa, perfected the technique of long-distance manufacturing. Meanwhile, Mexico turned its attention from internal economic development to luring international investment.

"For the Mexican government, the revenue from maquiladora production is pivotal," said Shaiken. "Maquiladoras furnish the second-largest source of foreign exchange for the Mexican economy (after oil). That creates a culture in which anything favoring the maquiladora production is emphasized, while the human cost is not addressed."

In other words, Mexico created an economy dependent on a vast supply of low-wage workers. The only way to boost that economy is to increase the number of foreign companies operating factories in Mexico—boosting wages actually hurts the economy.

The profits from that economy go two places—to foreign businesses and to the Mexican government. Neither has an incentive to improve workers' lives.

The threat from cheaper Latin American countries and China could have pushed the Mexican government to plow its maquiladora profits into developing home-grown industries that wouldn't move. Instead, Mexico is desperately—and ultimately vainly—attempting to keep its maquiladoras.

"They're promoting a policy of fear, in which workers are told it's better to see five pesos in wages cut to three than to lose their jobs entirely," said Martha Ojeda, director of the Coalition for Justice in the Maquiladoras. "If we don't accept the reform, the companies say they'll take their investment elsewhere.

Alarmed by the loss of jobs to China, Mexico President Vincente Fox promised to provide foreign companies with "China-like

Many families of workers in foreign-owned factories in Juárez live in fetid slums. One expert calls it high-productivity poverty."

conditions" in Mexico, a suggestion that sent shudders through labor lawyer Terrazas.

"If Fox were here I would say 'Listen, fucker, workers need more pay not less pay,'" Terrazas said. "Stop thinking about China and think about Mexico."

It's difficult to avoid thinking about China in Juárez, where crime and poverty rise and fall with a global economy over which residents have no control.

Frank Noble, a 19-year veteran of the KenSa plant in Harbor Beach was in Juárez in summer 2004 training workers who would eventually replace him. At a souvenir stand, he bought a Mexican-style blanket, ashtrays and ceramic trinkets for his co-workers in Michigan.

All were made in China.

"I thought, what is going on?" Noble said. "If they can't keep this stuff, they're in trouble, too."

Caught in trap of price-cutting moves

Mexican workers saved KenSa, but company owner Hal Zaima wondered if he needed to lay them off to save it again.

His decision to move several hundred Michigan jobs to Mexico in 2000 was painful and unpopular, but it kept his company afloat.

In 2004, auto companies demanded more price cuts. He had space in Honduras for more workers at half the price of his Mexican employees. But Mexican law required KenSa to pay laid-off workers 90 days' pay.

Would the savings in salary in Honduras make up for the layoff pay in Mexico?

It was a cruel calculation, one that would affect hundreds of lives.

"I don't make the rules," Zaima said. "I just play the game."

It's a game with fewer and fewer moves for owners and workers. Auto suppliers, which make more than half of a vehicle's components, bear the brunt of the cost-cutting efforts of the Big Three. Automakers now routinely demand 5 percent annual price cuts from suppliers. In its 2000 restructuring, Chrysler insisted on 15 percent price concessions from its parts suppliers.To offset the cuts, component manufacturers have struggled to increase productivity, but their profit margins continue to narrow. Now, suppliers face the added burden of sharply rising raw material costs.

Workers in Mexico are learning what those in Harbor Beach already know—their future depends less on the quality of their work than the size of their paychecks.

Many reasons to leave, few to stay

Today, there is a glut of workers in Juárez. Companies that recruited workers from 1,000 miles away a few years ago now have the opposite problem. "We'll put an ad in for 20 workers, and by 6 a.m. there'll be 100 people waiting at the door," Robles said.

The pay hikes and benefits given to workers during the worker shortage can't be taken back. Though there are no unions, Mexican law prohibits companies from taking away benefits they've previously given to workers.

Farmers with worn-out land and economic refugees from the poorest states of Mexico—Oaxaca, Veracruz and Durango—continue to flood into Juárez looking for work even while factories close. In four years, the population of Juárez has jumped by 200,000, to 1.4 million, while factory jobs dropped by 55,000.

Leading the exodus are wire harness manufacturers. Mexico still manufactures 78 percent of wire harnesses imported to the United States, but its market share is slipping.

Companies that moved jobs from the U.S. have been even quicker to pull out of Mexico, both because there is no political fallout from moving out of Mexico and because they do not face the constraints of labor contracts. Usually the factories themselves are leased, making it even easier to skip the country.

"We've created a higher-paid work force, which is becoming less competitive, which forces jobs to move," said Charlie Hill, KenSa plant manager in Juárez.

Hill has worked in wire harness factories in Michigan, Mississippi, Texas and Mexico. He's seen the industry shift before, and he feels the factory floor beneath him moving again.

"Mexico cannot compete with Honduras as far as labor goes,"

Hill said. "But it can compete with technology and with the education of the work force. Mexico's strong point is that it's been making wiring harnesses here since '72. The labor force is highly skilled at building wiring harnesses. It's like a family—everybody knows everybody."

It's the same argument used in vain for a decade to keep jobs in the United States.

Mexico took Michigan's mass-manufactured wire harness industry in the 1990s. Now, Mexico is taking the small, special-order wire harness industry from that state. Instead of making thousands of battery cables per order for Chrysler minivans, the Mexican plant may produce a few hundred wiring harnesses per order for the replacement market.

There is pain in Hill's voice as he talks of the transition. For a brief but shining moment, the Juárez plant was the company's savior; now it seems the next likely victim as other factories, in other lands, offer deliverance.

"You've got to go someplace," Hill said. "(But) the same thing will happen in Honduras someday."

For now, the buses keep rolling through Juárez, albeit with more empty seats.

There is a Mexican saying familiar to workers that sums up the Juárez experience, Terrazas said:

"So close to the United States, so far from God." At dusk, another bus from a factory pulls into Anapra, its shocks squeaking as it rocks through potholes filled with sewage.

"I see all this and I want to cry," Terrazas said.

PROFILE: ANA AGUILAR

Woman leaves home, family behind in search of a better life
Ana Lilia Maldenado Aguilar is one of the lucky ones. She and her husband still have jobs in the factories. They rent a small, well-kept home. They hope to buy a used car this winter.

Yet she misses her home in Veracruz, a thousand miles away from this dusty factory town. Her father died since she moved here. Her mother is alone. But Aguilar hasn't gone home since she moved here two years ago because she can't afford the bus ticket to visit.

"I want to cry," she said. "I want to save money."

At the KenSa wire harness factory in Juárez, Aguilar earns $54 a week. That's more than she could earn in Veracruz, but far less than she'd make on the other side of the Rio Grande, in the United States. There, workers at a warehouse storing wire harnesses made at Aguilar's plant earn more than $300 per week.

That's the paradox of the American dream, Mexican-style: the better things get, the clearer it becomes that things aren't good enough.

"I make more money here (than in Veracruz)," said Aguilar, 28. "But not enough. I cannot survive on less money."

Each workday, Aguilar gets on a bus at 5 a.m. for the trip to the factory. She returns $11\frac{1}{2}$ hours later, walking the last few blocks through what passes for a subdivision in Juárez—cinder block homes in cheery hues of yellow, green and purple, with faux window shutters.

Aguilar and her husband share a home that is smaller than many American family rooms. The floor is poured concrete. A washing machine sits outside the back door in a small, dirt back yard separated from neighboring yards by a 3-foot wall.

The couple rents the home for $18 per week. It's a fancier lifestyle than she grew up with, but she's also less satisfied. In Juárez, there is always something just out of reach.

Aguilar and her husband are trying to save money to buy a car, because their home is a bus ride away from any type of store. They dream of buying a home, but, with their combined salaries from the factories, that seems out of reach.

"This is our home now," Aguilar said. "We will stay here. But I would like to make more money."

She knows American factories came to Mexico because people like her work cheap. She also knows that some of those American factories are going to other countries now, where people will work for even less.

She says she doesn't worry about losing her job to Honduras or China.

"I hope that doesn't happen," Aguilar said. "I don't think about that. I'm happy to have a job."

Ana Aguilar walks through her neighborhood.
She is lucky—she and her husband, who works at another factory,
can afford to rent a spartan home about the size
of an American family room.

CHAPTER FIVE

SAN PEDRO SULA, HONDURAS

The overheated crowd stirs as two Americans approach the gate. Faces push through iron bars, shouting and smiling to draw the attention of the men they hope are offering jobs.

Fanny Soyepa Mejia slips to the front of the crowd. She arrived at the industrial park at 7 a.m. Five hours later, it is 100 degrees under a baking tropical sun, but the 28-year-old refuses to leave. Today, she hopes, might be the day she gets a factory job.

She hasn't worked in three years. She has four sons and no husband, and no way to pay the 20 lempiras ($1.11) per month to send each of her kids to school.

Some days, personnel directors inside the gate tell the guards to pick people for job interviews. There are always more people outside than jobs inside.

"I want to work," Mejia says. "I am a hard worker."

There are 300 at the gate, mostly women. They squeeze Mejia tight against the bars as guards with pistols split the mob for an incoming car. Juan Howlet steers his sedan slowly through the throng, heading for the KenSa wire harness factory inside the industrial park.

"This is the story every morning," said the plant manager, waving at the crowd. "They need jobs. This country needs jobs."

Central America is the new Mexico. Its poorer and less-developed countries are now a prime destination for American jobs. U.S. companies now rush to open factories in Honduras, El Salvador and Guatemala, seeking cheaper workers than can be found in Juárez.

By 2004, Yazaki North America, a branch of the Japanese wire harness manufacturer Yazaki Corp., had 3,800 employees in Nicaragua. Lear Corp. had about 4,000 workers outside San Pedro Sula in Honduras. Alcoa Fujikura had 500 workers 18 miles down the road, in El Progresso.

In April, 2004 KenSa started production in a rented, temporary facility in San Pedro Sula while a new factory was built. It hired 150 workers to make Chrysler minivan door wire harnesses at the Honduran minimum wage of about 55 cents an hour. It turned hundreds of people away.

No economic miracle

From the window of an airplane descending into San Pedro Sula, Hal Zaima could see the lush hillsides and broad coffee and banana plantations of Honduras. When he landed and climbed into his rental car, he saw a far different country.

Businessmen sometimes are kidnapped on the highway near the airport. The McDonald's along the road into town has a guard at the door brandishing a shotgun.

"You see people get straw and mud and try to put a building together, and that is their home," Zaima said. "You see people walking with huge buckets to the river, and that is their water for cooking and washing."

APRIL
2004
KenSa
FACTORY JOBS
USA: 80 MEXICO: 250 HONDURAS: 110

Honduras is one of the poorest and least-developed countries in Latin America. Nearly two-thirds of Hondurans live in poverty, according to the World Bank, with a per-capita annual income of $930.

There is one bright spot in the economy: foreign-owned factories. This country the size of Ohio has the third highest number of foreign-owned factories in the world, with 110,000 employees in 2002. More than one in five jobs in Honduras now is in the factories. For many, it is the first time they've earned a steady income.

While the income is steady, it is dismally low.

"They (Honduran factory workers) probably are better off than what they'd be in the non-maquiladora economy," said Andrew Schrank, assistant professor of sociology and Latin American studies at Yale, who specializes in the study of foreign-owned factories. "But just because working in a factory is better than working in the fields doesn't mean that a maquiladora job is a good job, by American standards or even international standards."

Most workers at foreign-owned factories in Honduras make $4.44 a day. That's less than the historic $5 a day Henry Ford paid his Highland Park, Michigan workers 90 years ago, in 1914. Ford's pay (the equivalent of $11 an hour today) more than doubled the minimum wage at the time and helped give birth to America's blue-collar middle class.

Ford wasn't being generous. He believed that paying his workers enough to afford the vehicles they built would increase profits. The economy of the industrial Midwest was built on good wages for assembly line work and the loyalty of workers and their extended families buying the vehicles they built.

U.S. companies have no such incentive in countries such as Honduras. Products are built for export back to America. Raising worker salaries in San Pedro Sula won't sell even one more SUV in Detroit.

Factory workers in Honduras don't own cars. Imported vehicles with parking stickers in the windows from their original homes in New Jersey, Florida or Ohio rattle along roads lined with ragtag children selling fruit in small bags. Fruit trees are everywhere. In some ways the Hondurans are better off than their peers in the desert factory town of Juárez. Hondurans can eat all the bananas they can stomach. But many go weeks without meat or a substantial amount of rice.

"Most of these workers are at most a generation away from an agricultural lifestyle," Schrank said. "In all of Latin America, the real poverty is in the countryside. It (factory work) is a step up, but it's a step up from real poverty."

For Hondurans, working for U.S. bosses is nothing new. Honduras was the quintessential "banana republic" in the first half of the

1900s, with bananas providing 66 percent of the country's exports and U.S. companies owning 75 percent of the fields. These powerful companies—supported by U.S. troops on occasion— were partly responsible for the development of Honduras' oppressive military and government.

Today, there is virtually no middle class in Honduras. The nation has one of the broadest inequities of wealth distribution in the world. Yet there are few complaints from factory workers, who in some cases earn too little to buy clean drinking water. In Honduras, there is always someone who has even less.

Coveted jobs barely pay enough money to survive

Sara Isabel Pena Diaz first saw a wire harness in May 2004. Trainers at the new factory explained that the long cords of wire were destined for new automobiles in the United States. Touching the strips of copper and plastic was the closest Diaz had ever come to a new car, or to the country she idolized.

The diminutive 30-year-old wraps electrical tape around bundles of wires eight hours a day for KenSa. Of the 520 lempiras she earns a week, 125 pays for bus fare to and from work, and another 100 covers groceries. That leaves the equivalent of about $16 a week for all other expenses.

"I am dreaming the American Dream," Diaz said. "I dream of making more money."

American companies have exported jobs, but not the lifestyles those jobs supported in the U.S. Unlike Mexico in the 1990s, there is no worker shortage to drive up salaries and benefits. Having learned a costly lesson in Mexico, companies do not provide transportation or meals. There are no bonuses for attendance or punc-

*Hundreds of people press against the gate
of an industrial park outside San Pedro Sula, Honduras,
hoping to be picked for jobs at the factories inside.*

tuality, though Honduran law requires factories to pay workers $6\frac{1}{2}$ days' salary for each five-day workweek.

Even with the extra day-and-a-half salary, Diaz's paycheck feels like a five-foot rope given to someone in a 10-foot hole.

"We barely survive," Diaz said through a translator. "We have to borrow for food and for child care. I have a baby who needs an eye operation, but I cannot afford it.

"I take things to the pawn shop. I've sold jewelry, rings. I sold my TV. Soon, I will run out of things to sell."

Yet ask Diaz about her job and she beams. She works in a clean, brightly lit factory instead of toiling in the broiling sun cutting sugar cane or avoiding robbers as a street vendor. As desperate as her life is, it would be worse without KenSa.

And that is the paradox of offshoring's impact in many countries. Should companies like KenSa be excoriated for not paying a living wage to its foreign workers? Or should the company be praised for providing jobs where none existed?

In Honduras, the factories act not as an economic ladder for its workers, but as a plug in a very leaky dike.

Someday wages may rise, when the Honduran economy improves or when enough companies move to the country to create a labor shortage. Then Diaz will make more money.

Or she might make none at all.

The factories came here because labor was cheap. Neighboring Nicaragua has cheaper labor than Honduras. Across the Pacific, workers in China, Indonesia and Vietnam will work for even less. Developing countries around the world have jumped on the Mexican bandwagon, ditching economic policies that encouraged national development for a policy that promotes the "rental" of cheap labor. The paychecks offered by foreign-owned factories prop up moribund economies but provide little investment for the future. Once the factories leave, the economy goes into a freefall Thus, the threat of jobs moving to even cheaper labor markets keeps a lid on the meager wages offered in the factories of Honduras.

"The mere fact that you get your foot on the lower rung doesn't mean you climb the ladder," Schrank said.

Countries like Honduras are being "squeezed from both sides," Schrank said. "What they don't realize is there are 15 countries behind them doing the same thing they are.

"South Korea has the high (technology) sector. Perhaps Mexico has the middle. And there are countries below Honduras that will build simple things for less."

*New workers at the KenSa plant in Honduras gather for a training session.
Workers in developing countries, many of whom have never before
worked in factories, make more errors than do workers in the United States.
But at a wage of less than $5 a day, they're still a better
deal for their American bosses.*

Honduran textile workers are learning that lesson today. More than 60 percent of the country's manufactured exports are textiles and apparel made in foreign-owned factories. When trade barriers to Chinese textiles were lifted in the U.S. in 2005, clothing from China flooded America, replacing clothing from Latin America. As textile maquiladoras close, the pool of desperate workers in Honduras grows, further depressing wages.

In 2004, Zaima spoke with affection for his employees in Honduras. Zaima hoped that when a permanent facility was finished in 2005, he could increase employment from 150 to 800 workers. But when he talked of long-term expansion, he talked of China.

And just in case he needs to move again, Zaima made sure to only lease the property.

What used to be a brick-and-mortar business had become a mobile home business. Zaima joked about factories on wheels, but many Americans weren't laughing.

Grateful for jobs others lost

An August 2004 Gallup Poll found that 61 percent of Americans worry that their jobs or the jobs of their family or friends will be shipped to another country. Lou Dobbs rails nightly on CNN on the evils of offshoring. Stories of slump-shouldered employees boxing up their factory equipment for shipment to a new plant in Mexico are a water cooler cliché. Businessmen who ship jobs overseas have made politicians and used-car salesmen look popular.

"It seems sleazy on the surface," Schrank said. "Is it a noble way to do business? It seems unseemly to be constantly chasing the cheapest worker."

Zaima chafes at the bloodless caricature of businessmen like himself. Yes, he has put a lot of Americans on the unemployment line, Zaima admits. But he's helped hundreds of others around the world who are even more desperate for jobs.

He recalls a June 2004 trip to Honduras, when workers lined up to hug him to thank him for their jobs. One by one, the Hondurans approached the American, wrapping their arms around him.

"Most of the time, I only get bad news," Zaima said later. "I had this warm feeling. It was the best experience I've ever had in a plant."

It was a bittersweet moment for Diaz, knowing she is sinking farther in debt, but also knowing how much faster those outside the gate are sinking.

"If everything stays like this, my life will get worse," Diaz said. "(But) I feel pity for the people outside (the gate), and it makes me love my job more."

Outside the gate, Mejia discovers there will be no job today.

She'll go home and get some rest. Tomorrow morning, she'll be up early again to return to the gate.

PROFILE: JORGE RUIZ PUERTO

Honduran man turns to faith as his income drops

Jorge Ruís Puerto made more money selling mangoes door to door.

But his truck, a 1984 Nissan, broke down and repairs cost $500. It might as well be $5,000.

Puerto works at a wire harness factory, a clean, new facility inside the gates of an industrial park, where he earns 90 lempiras a day. Honduran law requires that KenSa give workers 6.5 days' pay for each five-day workweek. With that extra pay, Puerto's effective salary is about 81 cents an hour.

"I don't have enough income to support all I need," Puerto said through a translator. "(But) the economy is bad. There are no jobs."

The 41-year-old is lucky. Many factories don't hire anyone over age 25. And as is the case in Mexico and China, women make up the majority of wire harness employees in Honduras.

Puerto knows it could be worse. But he also knows that his children often are hungry.

Puerto moves inventory around the factory. At the end of his shift, he rides his bicycle to a home built by hand from abandoned cinder blocks. He lives in the small home with his wife, niece and three children.

He buys clean water for his children to drink. He drinks and bathes in water he keeps in a bucket outside the home. He cleans himself with a hard block of laundry soap.

When he sold fruit out of his truck, he had enough money to take his family to Pizza Hut once every month or two. Those trips are gone. A typical dinner at Puerto's home today is beans, tortillas and a small piece of cheese.

"What I feel most is the (loss of) food," Puerto said. "Milk, meat, cheese, everything is so expensive. I used to eat better."

Puerto blames the government for setting the minimum wage at the factories low, in order to attract companies from Mexico.

"The pay at the (factories) is very low," Puerto said. "I have to stay at this job because I have responsibilities with my family. I have to be thankful for what I have."

When told some factory workers in the U.S. make 20 to 30 times more money than him, Puerto shrugs. "Anyone wants to get more money for the value of their work," he said. "But you can't do anything about the situation. I'd have to move to another country."

Puerto's wife is a school teacher, earning almost twice as much

Jorge Ruís Puerto holds his son outside the home he built by hand out of discarded cinderblocks. He makes too little money at the U.S. factory to afford basics like clean drinking water and soap.

as him. But the Honduran government hasn't paid its teachers in seven months. She keeps working without getting paid, knowing that's the only chance she has of getting at least some of her back pay.

"It is hard times," Puerto said. "I have faith God will help me with these problems."

Each night after work, Puerto walks to the Renovacion Carismatica Catolica Church. Sometimes he prays, sometimes he visits people who are sick.

He opened a well-worn Bible to his favorite passage, Luke 12:22: ". . . do not worry about your life, what you will eat; or about your body, what you will wear. Life is more than food, and the body more than clothes."

His faith has grown as his income has dropped. "God has shown me not to just rely on material things," he said.

At night, he leaves the church and walks to the bus stop to wait for his wife. It is too dangerous for her to walk home alone.

CHAPTER SIX

WUHU, CHINA

The American businessmen raised their glasses for yet another toast.

For hours, they sampled steaming bowls of turtle, frog, shrimp, duck feet and raw fish of every size and facial expression. Zhifu Shen, vice president of Tianhai Electric Co., had shown his new business partners how to eat cake with chopsticks. Every few minutes, Zhifu offered another toast of Maotai, a strong rice schnapps.

Even without the alcohol, the past three days had been disorienting for KenSa executives John Nye and John Clough. They struggled with jet lag and unfamiliar food. They'd spent days poring over financial spreadsheets translated on the fly. They were tired and off-balance, struggling to keep up in an upside-down world.

The Americans and Chinese both had reasons to celebrate. Zhifu was selling controlling interest of a wire harness plant in Wuhu to the Michigan company, giving Tianhai Electric a shot of cash and the promise of American manufacturing expertise. In return, KenSa was getting 250 Chinese workers who, combined, would be paid less than the company's 15 remaining assembly workers in Michigan.

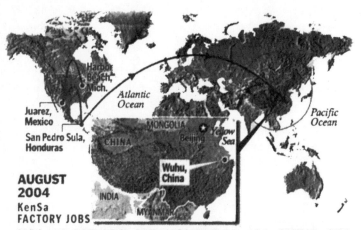

Juarez, Mexico

San Pedro Sula, Honduras

AUGUST 2004
KenSa
FACTORY JOBS

USA: 15 MEXICO: 225 HONDURAS: 150 **CHINA: 250**

Clough, KenSa's chief financial officer, and Nye, director of operations, had traversed 12 time zones to ask Chinese workers to make the same product that Michigan workers had made for decades. The Chinese factory wasn't as efficient. Distribution was a headache. The workers made more errors than the veteran employees in Michigan. But the Chinese workers did something the Harbor Beach workers could never do—they worked a full day for the cost of a Starbucks Frappuccino.

Low costs in China send suppliers scrambling

Wuhu is a gray industrial town in Anhui province, a four-hour train trip from Shanghai across rice fields and fish ponds. Yet the Conch International Hotel is filled nightly with guests from Germany, Australia, Japan and the United States.

They don't come for sightseeing or to sample the salty duck

heads on the breakfast buffet. They carry laptops and briefcases, and they wait impatiently in the hotel lobby for their translators so they can visit their factories.

In a city the size of Columbus, Ohio, there were 104 factories owned or partly owned by foreign companies in 2004, up from 55 just five years earlier.

Germany-based Siemens AG builds automotive gauges in Wuhu; Tower Automotive, based in Troy, Michigan, builds suspension components.

Wuhu is one of dozens of industrial centers in China, which has become a Candyland for Rust Belt manufacturers hungry for cheap labor. Some factories pay workers the equivalent of 30 cents an hour, with few of the benefits received by American or even Mexican employees. China is investing billions of dollars in road projects, making the movement of products easier than in many developing countries. And the government, albeit one of the last Communist strongholds in the world, is stable and business-friendly.

Emerging from decades of isolation, China has opened its market to foreign automakers in the hopes they will help transform its eclectic jumble of 300-odd vehicle manufacturers into a world-class industry. Both Ford and GM produce cars in China with local partners. They also have opened major purchasing offices in Shanghai to buy billions of dollars worth of Chinese-made components.

Many suppliers moved to China to feed auto parts to Chinese assembly plants of U.S.- and other foreign-based automakers, which were jostling for their share of the country's exploding auto market.

Michigan-based Delphi Corporation alone has invested more than $400 million, opening 11 factories in China since 1991 and building a $15 million research and development center in Shanghai.

Low wages, minimal environmental standards and a fixed-rate currency have made Chinese auto parts dirt cheap.

Once suppliers were established in China, exporting back to the United States made financial sense.

"You can't blame the auto companies," said Christopher Kirsch, general manager of Interstate Tool & Dye Company, a Madison Heights auto supplier that has gone out of business partly because of international competition. "If you're in a purchasing position at a car company, and you get rewarded for saving your company money, why wouldn't you buy overseas?"

KenSa had already moved most of its production from Michigan to Mexico just four years before. The company was still working out of a temporary facility in Honduras while a new factory was built there. While Zaima thought the company might open a factory in China someday, nobody in the summer of 2003 in KenSa's small management staff was ready to move.

Bo Andersson had different ideas.

In a meeting of General Motors suppliers in 2003, Andersson, the powerful vice president of worldwide purchasing for GM, named the price that the automaker would pay for wire harnesses in China, according to several executives in attendance. Anyone who wanted to do business with GM should plan to meet that price, Andersson declared.

The Big Three had quietly suggested suppliers move overseas to save money for years. But the bluntness of Andersson's statement caught the businessmen off-guard.

Zaima did not attend the meeting, but word spread quickly among suppliers. "I thought we'd better accelerate our plans," he said later. "I didn't think it was coming this fast."

A row of employees cut wires for wiring harnesses at a factory in Wuhu, China. Workers earn as little as 45 cents an hour.

China has changed more than the price of wire harnesses. It has become the benchmark for automakers as they determine what they will pay for parts.

"(The automakers) hit them over the head with China pricing," said Kim Hill, assistant director of the Economics and Business Group at the Center for Automotive Research in Ann Arbor. "When they talk to a supplier, they want to see evidence of a China component."

Even if two suppliers offer the same price for a product and one builds the part in China, "they'll go to the other supplier and say, 'How much could you lower your price if you were in China?'" Hill said. "You have to justify not being in China."

Today, GM imports only one-tenth of 1 percent of parts used in U.S. assembly plants from China (Michigan factories supply 14 percent). But the company expects to increase its auto part purchases from China to its factories around the globe 20-fold in six years—from $200 million in 2003 to $4 billion in 2009.

If offshoring one-tenth of 1 percent of auto parts to China is costing thousands of jobs in Michigan, former KenSa owner Kathy Goheen shudders at what will happen as outsourcing increases.

"I keep hoping I'll live long enough to see this exodus to other countries turn around," Goheen said. "But greed is a terrible thing."

"China is setting a lot of things in motion," Hill said. "(Auto companies) ask for global pricing. That's code for China."

So Clough and Nye trundled off to the Conch International Hotel in Wuhu, waving hello to some of the same businessmen they'd met in other hotels in other countries.

But China wasn't Mexico or Honduras. China was the other side of the world in more ways than one, and business was not ever going to be the same.

Here, four-lane freeways turned to dirt paths and back again. Ox carts mingled in traffic jams with minivans. High-rise apartments overlooked rice paddies. And in Wuhu, American businessmen jammed into a hotel featuring virulently anti-American art of the Statue of Liberty on fire.

From farms to factories, a cultural revolution

Huang Wei loves Britney Spears. She sings American pop songs at the local karaoke. She talks on a cell phone with friends about boys and clothes and the Americans she's seen recently in her factory.

"All the workers know the Americans bought into the company," the 22-year-old said through a translator. "The workers think it is a good thing. They look forward to a better future."

KenSa employees work to translate Chinese documents into English
as they consider buying a factory in China.

Huang earned $22.50 a week cutting and bundling wires eight hours a day, almost twice as much as she earned as a school teacher.

In summer 2004, KenSa was negotiating to purchase controlling interest of the plant. American-owned factories often have marginally better pay and working conditions than Chinese-owned plants. This is especially true among auto supply companies, where high worker turnover can lower quality.

Still, the same product that allowed workers in the United States to buy two-story homes didn't allow Chinese workers to rent an apartment.

KenSa's 250 workers earn between 45 cents and 60 cents an hour. Huang lives with her parents, a short electric scooter ride past sampan houseboats from KenSa. It is a tidy if Spartan home, with poured concrete floors and brightly painted, unadorned walls.

Most don't have that option. The majority of factory workers migrate from villages hundreds of miles away. They travel to Wuhu, a regional industrial center, looking for work much as immigrants traveled to Detroit a century ago. Some share small apartments. About 40 KenSa employees live in dormitories on the first floor of the factory.

There are eight bunks per room. Some bunks have mosquito netting. One worker taped a newspaper page on the wall above her pillow to personalize her space.

When not working on the factory floor or sleeping in their un-air-conditioned dorm rooms, workers congregate in a large room that serves both as a dining hall and lounge. Folding chairs are set up in rows in front of a television, which seems to always be airing some kind of kung-fu soap opera. There is a ping-pong table. In a small kitchen, large pots are filled with rice for dinner.

Sometimes, workers ride a bus or bicycle to downtown Wuhu, where they can stroll past the clothing, jewelry and cell phone shops lining the city's pedestrian mall. Window-shopping is about all they can do. A meal out at the trendy Kentucky Fried Chicken can cost more than a day's wages. A shirt can cost a week's salary.

And the cars in which the wiring harnesses they build are installed? The cheapest new cars would cost KenSa assembly line workers at least six years' salary.

Wang Chunhei, 24, shared a dorm room with seven other young men, all of whom came from villages where the salaries in Wuhu sounded like a fortune. At night, the men talked about cars and girls and the life that was out there beyond the factory walls, close enough that they could almost taste it. Wang's living conditions were better than his parents', but "the salary is not high enough," he said. "The cost of living is higher here."

Since laws prohibiting peasants from moving to cities were relaxed in the late 1980s, between 60 million and 130 million people—as much as 10 percent of the country's population—have migrated to cities like Wuhu. Most moved to work in factories.

Many are young single women. They are dagongmei, peasant working girls whom city residents look down upon. They blame the dagongmei for a crime wave. The factory workers, in turn, say city residents are unfriendly.

"A lot of the migrants I talk to find that conditions are pretty terrible and pay is very low, but they're happy to be in a big city with some sense of freedom," said Mary Gallagher, a University of Michigan professor who studies Chinese labor issues in Shanghai.

But what happens when workers tire of living in dorms?

It's not a pressing question for young workers in China's factories, struggling to scratch out a living.

Huang is surprised to hear her job may have until recently belonged to an American. She doesn't feel bad because "Americans are rich" and don't need jobs.

Like past generations of blue-collar workers half a world away, Huang believes she controls her future, that her factory job is hers to keep as long as she works hard.

A young woman of the provinces, Huang isn't attuned to the market forces that placed a wire cutter in her hand and a paycheck in her purse.

But back in Harbor Beach, workers have seen abstract market forces shred their lives. They've become students of world economics and paid for the lesson with their jobs.

They whisper about tariffs and exchange rates instead of sports. They exchange rumors of layoffs in Mexico and hirings in Honduras, and analyze what it could mean to them.

They've learned the hard lesson taught in towns across the Rust Belt—everyone is replaceable.

Huang doesn't believe it. "I cannot say I like it, but I have adjusted to factory life," she said. "I feel very proud of my job. I'm confident that no one can replace me."

Looking for a cheaper China

Zhifu He wants to replace Huang.

"Wages in China are going up," said Zhifu, Tianhai Electric's general manager. "We are concerned about this problem."

Even in China, factories are moving to find cheaper labor in land away from the more expensive coast.

In Shanghai, where GM's biggest ventures are based, wages are four times higher than they are in Chongqing, where Ford builds vehicles with a Chinese partner.

Tianhai has five wire harness factories around China (KenSa bought the controlling interest of one, in Wuhu). "For the wages of a worker in Shanghai, we can pay two workers in Wuhu, or three workers in Hunan province," Zhifu said. "There is a big gap (in wages) between the cities and the interior."

Tianhai is building a new factory in Xiangtan City in Hubei province, where wages will be substantially less than the 45 cents to 60 cents an hour earned in Wuhu.

"It is very critical to manage expense," Zhifu said.

The Chinese businessman has heard Americans complain about losing jobs to China. "Why do Americans feel they are entitled to

Huang Wei rides her electric scooter to the factory.
Wei is part of a generation of Chinese moving from
rural China to the nation's cities to work in foreign factories.

jobs?" he asked. "When they have jobs, (U.S.) workers complain to their superiors. I cannot understand it.

"American people have a sense of superiority," Zhifu said. "They think they're better than Chinese people. Chinese people are different. They want to look for opportunity to change. This is very realistic."

At the dinner, the Chinese businessman and his American counterparts raised glass after glass in celebration. The hangover may be felt in America for years.

"Chinese workers will take American jobs," Zhifu said. "This is the reality of the market economy. If the American people don't want to go out to look for opportunity and Chinese people want to go out, then it is America's problem."

PROFILE: WANG MIN

45-cent-an-hour job gives woman hope for future

Wang Min lives in a small dormitory room with seven other factory workers. She doesn't know how she could ever afford a car in which the wire harnesses she builds are installed. She isn't even sure what the bundles of wires do.

But she does know one thing: she's happy with the job that pays her about 45 cents per hour.

Wang, 20, grew up in Henan Province, a beautiful but impoverished region known as the cradle of Chinese culture. At 17, she paid a factory the equivalent of nine weeks' salary just to be allowed to work—a common practice in rural China, where there are millions more people than jobs. The charge was considered a "deposit"—if Wang worked at the factory for five years, she'd get her money back.

Few work there that long. Wang sewed men's suits for 300 yuan ($36.50) a month—about 23 cents an hour. She shared a room the size of a walk-in closet with three women, located directly above the factory's boiler.

"It was very bad, very hot," Wang said through a translator.

She quit after eight months. Hearing there were jobs available in Wuhu, Wang traveled 600 miles by train—the equivalent of Detroit to Chattanooga, Tennessee—for a better-paying job. At Tianhai Electric Corp., she is paid the equivalent of $18 per week—$21 when she works overtime.

Wang pays $1.20 per month to live in the factory dormitory, a barren room with four bunk beds. Some beds have mosquito netting over them. Others have cardboard beneath the mattresses for support. Her roommates are all young women like her, who traveled from China's vast interior looking for a better life.

Wang thinks she's found it. She works during the day and watches TV and shares "girl talk" with her roommates at night. They talk about cosmetics and clothes and marriage. She reads romance novels. Occasionally, she pulls out a Chinese/English dictionary and memorizes another word in English.

Someday, she'd like to go to college and learn English. That, she says, would help her in her career.

For now, she is happy making wire harnesses, especially now that an American company has purchased her factory. Workers say Americans are better bosses, more willing to raise their pay and listen to their complaints.

Wang Min earns 45 cents an hour—not enough to rent an apartment. She sleeps in a bunk bed in a room with eight women inside the factory.

Wang has little sense of her role in a churning global economy. She doesn't know why American companies are coming to China, and is unaware that she is taking the job of an American worker.

"America is a rich country," Wang said. "Workers who lose jobs at a factory can get a job at another factory."

Wang also has no idea of the difference in pay. She guesses that American workers doing the same work as her may get paid twice as much as her. In reality, a UAW worker would get almost 50 times more.

"I am very satisfied with my work," Wang said. "I will continue to do my best."

CHAPTER SEVEN

HARBOR BEACH REDUX

In her nightmare, Deb Coverdill was in her car. "I'm dressed and I'm driving to work," Coverdill said. "I'm driving and I'm driving and I'm driving, and I never get there."

She awoke in a sweat. She still has a job, she told herself, she still has a job.

The 46-year-old had survived round after round of layoffs at KenSa by October 2004, but her future was still in doubt. Owner Hal Zaima called the factory a "stepchild" to his offshore operations, warning workers that the plant would close unless he could sell it.

Shuttering the plant would surprise no one. It had been an era of upheaval and soul-searching, and lying awake in bed, Coverdill turned to God for an answer.

"Please let us keep our jobs," she prayed. "Please let things work out at the plant."

At 10:45 p.m. on November 2, 2004, her prayers were answered. After weeks of negotiations, Zaima signed a contract to sell the factory and its assets.

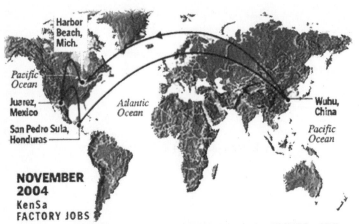

NOVEMBER 2004
KenSa
FACTORY JOBS
USA: 0 MEXICO: 210 HONDURAS: 110 CHINA: 175

The new owner was A.G. Manufacturing, a company formed for the purchase by a group of auto industry consultants. One of the new owners, Victor Edozien, visited the plant days earlier, assuring workers that he had big plans for the factory.

The Harbor Beach employees were cautious. After seeing so many jobs go overseas, they weren't sure if this auto industry consultant offered them a fresh start or just a stay of execution. Yet when word leaked onto the factory floor on November 3 that the papers had been signed, Coverdill felt a twinge of something rare and precious in her hometown: optimism.

"He said there were jobs out there, you just had to go get them," Coverdill said. "He said all the right things."

Stretching definition of an American company

Most Americans have never heard of Chery Automotive, but they will soon.

The 7-year-old Chinese automaker sold 100,000 vehicles in China in 2003 and 150,000 this year. By 2007, officials expect to sell 500,000 cars and export their inexpensive knockoffs of big-brand vehicles to the United States. The subcompact QQ sells for $6,725—about $3,500 less than Chevy's China-market Spark, of which the QQ is a nearly exact duplicate.

In a meeting at the automaker's Wuhu, China, headquarters in August 2004, purchasing director Tao Yuan complained that the wire harnesses Chery bought from Delphi's China branch cost too much.

John Clough, KenSa's CFO, knew why: Delphi had too many employees in the United States.

"As you know, the U.S. has very high labor costs," Clough told the potential customer. "We (KenSa) have a very small number of people in the U.S.

"Our goal," Clough said, "is to reduce our exposure to U.S. manufacturing."

That goal was accomplished. In November 2004, KenSa had about 130 employees in Honduras, 230 in Mexico, 250 in China and—in the wake of the factory sale—zero assembly workers in the U.S.

By 2008, if things go according to plan, the company will have 800 employees in Mexico, 1,000 in Honduras and at least 1,000 in China, stretching its designation as an American company.

KenSa will keep its headquarters in the Detroit suburb of Sterling Heights because "Detroit is still the heartbeat of the auto industry," Zaima said. But if Zaima's ambitious expansion plans come to fruition, about 40 workers, or less than 2 percent of the company's staff, will be in the United States.

Company executives will be based here, as well as some accountants, sales staff and engineers. But even they shouldn't get too comfortable.

"We plan to offshore some engineers," Zaima said. In fall 2004 he hired two Honduran engineers to work at KenSa's factory in San Pedro Sula. The salary for the college-educated engineers: $350 a month, or about $2.18 an hour.

"One of our customers said, 'You're in the right places—you guys are doing the right thing,' " Zaima said.

Consumers pay lower prices, watch stock values rise

The headlines about factories moving to China tell only part of the offshoring story, Zaima said. Globalization is bringing some jobs to the United States. In fall 2004, KenSa hired an engineer in its Sterling Heights office who speaks Chinese—the only U.S. employee who can communicate directly with KenSa's workers in China.

A study by the Economic Policy Institute found that Michigan lost 97,411 jobs overseas in the past decade, but also gained 45,945—a net loss, but not a total loss.

In the United States, globalization offers higher stock prices for the shareholders of companies moving overseas and lower prices for products ranging from roasters at Wal-Mart to SUVs at Big Three dealerships.

"At the end of the day, the biggest value we're getting (from globalization) is consumer products," said Zaima. "We're beneficiaries of cheap labor in other countries."

But even as he moves jobs overseas, Zaima sometimes wonders who will be left in America to buy those cheap products. "The chain is unraveling, and it was unraveled by us," Zaima said.

"The issue here isn't the present conditions for Mexican workers; it's the future conditions for workers" in the United States, said Shaiken, the University of California Berkeley professor.

Because auto suppliers must compete with the prices of suppliers in lower-cost countries, "salaries in Juárez exert a downward pressure on salaries in Warren (Michigan)," Shaiken said.

"We've seen the enemy," Zaima warned, "and it is us."

More Michigan layoffs, more soul searching

On Nov. 4, 2004, Deb Coverdill was laid off.

Nye broke the news to her. The new start promised by the new owner required fewer employees than expected, Nye said. The new owner wanted more employees let go before he took over.

The layoffs reduced the assembly-floor staff to about 10.

"I was speechless," Coverdill said. "I'd been there 19 years. I thought I was safe."

Weeks earlier, Coverdill had been offered a management position at the KenSa plant in Juárez, but the prospect of moving terrified Coverdill. "My whole family is here. I have a brand-new grandson. I have a son in his last two years of high school," Coverdill said. "I'd lose everything."

With no job, she risked losing her home. "I'm the main breadwinner in my house," Coverdill said. "That's why it hit me so hard."

Coverdill helped train the workers in Mexico and Honduras who replaced her and her friends. She doesn't blame them. But she can't help but feel anger toward Zaima.

"I like Hal, but he is very ambitious," Coverdill said. "He wants KenSa to be competitive with the Yazakis and the Lears (two of the world's largest wire harness manufacturers). And those plans didn't include Harbor Beach."

Zaima views his decisions less in terms of ambition than survival. "I hope somebody has a plan," he said, "because it's a lot bigger than me."

Like water flowing downhill, jobs move to the cheapest-labor countries. "In an incredibly brief moment in history, there has been a vast increase in the unskilled labor market," said Andrew Schrank, assistant professor of sociology of Latin American studies at Yale. "Think of women coming into the labor market in developing nations, plus agricultural mechanization that means fewer people are needed in the fields, plus the opening of China, where the vast majority of people still live off the land, plus the development of logistics to get products to market.

"To exhaust the supply of cheap labor could take not decades, but centuries."

In a kitchen in Deckerville, globalization is increasing the pressure on 12-year-old Cody and 14-year-old Brett to finish their homework.

Michigan KenSa worker Doug Ross is determined that his children go to college. "If you walk out of high school with a diploma and don't go to college, what are you going to get?" Ross asked. "You're going to end up working on a farm or in a factory in the same situation as me –wondering day to day in limbo about your job."

Ross accepted a job with AG Manufacturing at the former KenSa plant. If things go well, the factory may employ 50 people by 2007. Ross knows he's helpless to determine whether things go well.

"We're in a situation where any individual firm is powerless

94

to do much," Shaiken said. "If these are the norms we say are appropriate, we're looking at a future (in the U.S.) not only of lower wages, but of much lower purchasing power."

Already companies are looking for the next China. Yazaki has lobbied Congress to expand NAFTA to Haiti, where labor is cheaper than in Central America. Some regions of Africa would be even cheaper if governments were stable and transportation logistics could be solved.

"We'll probably end up in Antarctica someday," Nye joked.

Ross isn't laughing.

"I understand the reasons companies are going overseas," Ross said. "But I also have a problem with jobs being taken. I live here. I've got kids here. I want a good life, too."

Globalization fuels dreams and nightmares

Deb Coverdill and Huang Wei's lives continue to be connected. In China, Huang worked enough overtime recently to buy a cell phone. For the 22-year-old, it was a small but happy step toward something that even in her communist country is known as the American Dream.

"I am confident my life will improve with the company," Huang said through a translator.

Half a world away, Coverdill filled out job applications. She knew the chances of getting a job were slim, and the chances of getting a job that paid the $35,000 a year she made as quality control manager at KenSa were nil.

"I guess the free market helps people who are less fortunate, but eventually it has got to affect the United States," Coverdill said. "There's going to be nothing left here, or we're going to have to learn to live on a whole lot less income than what we're used to."

Coverdill still has trouble sleeping, but after she lost her job making wire harnesses, her prayers changed.

"Give me the strength to make it until I can find another job," she prays, "and help me remember that there are people who are worse off than me."

CHAPTER EIGHT

UPDATE

The story of Deb Coverdill, Huang Wei and hundreds of workers between them in the far-flung factories of KenSa won't settle the debate over globalization. In fact, there is plenty in their experiences to affirm the opinions of both critics and proponents of outsourcing.

When a version of this book ran in *The Detroit News* in November 2004, I was deluged with e-mails and telephone calls from people whose lives had been affected by globalization. A member of the United Auto Workers praised the article for illustrating how corporate America was screwing the hard-working men and women on the assembly line. The owner of a company that had shipped jobs overseas hailed the story for understanding that businesses have no choice. Perhaps the scariest e-mail came from a purchasing officer at one of the Big Three automakers, who said he'd gleaned ideas from the article on how to save his company more money by pushing suppliers offshore.

It's as if everyone posted the paragraphs reaffirming their beliefs on their refrigerators and stuffed the rest in the bottoms of bird cages.

But those beliefs were stood on their head just six months later. Coverdill was back at work at her American factory, while Huang had left her factory in China in the midst of layoffs.

For Coverdill, the time off had been hard on her and her family. She'd been called back to work two days a week in January by the new owner of the Harbor Beach plant, but the meager paychecks weren't enough to stave off bankruptcy.

"We lost a car," Coverdill said. "We lost everything but our house."

Called back to work full time in May 2005, she earned $19,000 a year instead of the $35,000 a year she made before her layoff. A friend of Coverdill's from the factory, John Hardy, who had survived round after round of layoffs, lost his job the day Coverdill regained hers.

"If I could do something else, I would," Coverdill said. "I'm doing twice the work for half the pay. But it's a new company and there's not a lot of work in this area."

There are times when Coverdill feels her life is frozen in amber, part of the last generation to make a decent living on the factory floor. "I think everybody is going to have to get used to a lower standard of living," Coverdill said.

Pain in China

While the U.S. worker regained her job, her Chinese counterpart, the optimistic Huang Wei, left the factory to work as a salesperson in a department store in Wuhu. The factory where she made automotive wire harnesses laid off most of its workers in the winter of 2004–05. Huang chose not to wait for her own layoff notice to find another job.

The layoffs were part of a ripple effect of the Chinese government decision to halt loans offered by state-run banks. The loan prohibition was an attempt to slow down an economy experts feared was growing too fast.

The factory's main customer, Chery Automotive, stopped its production line, leaving its parts suppliers with little work. Workers who months earlier felt their jobs were guaranteed were learning what their peers in the United States had known for years—no jobs are safe.

In May 2005, Huang worked seven hours a day, seven days a week as an assistant in the jewelry department of Shangzhidu department store. There, she sold necklaces and rings to Chinese who had scratched their way a few rungs up the economic ladder from the 22-year-old. Work behind the glass counters of the jewelry department was easier than that behind the machines on the factory floor, but Huang still could not survive on her own on her paycheck. The 45 cents an hour she earned at the department store—about the same as she earned at the wire harness factory—wasn't enough to allow her to move out of her parents' home into an apartment of her own.

Huang said she was "not very satisfied" with her job, describing her life in May 2005 as "a period of transition." It was a stunning admission for a woman who months earlier had expressed complete confidence in her economic future.

She doesn't want to spend her life as a sales clerk, and the events of the past year have made her wary of a future in the factory. Huang is scrimping to pay for night school classes in accounting, hoping they will get her closer to the American Dream.

The slowdown in the Chinese economy put the brakes on Ken-

Sa's plans there, also. In the summer of 2004, KenSa was negotiating to buy controlling interest of the Wuhu factory, with plans to employ 1,000 people by 2008.

By the summer of 2005, the company had yet to produce one wire harness in China, and the formerly gung ho KenSa owner Hal Zaima was now preaching caution.

"The honeymoon phase is over," Zaima said. "Some people are happy (in China) and some people are seeing the stark reality.

"There are too many dynamics working against you in China."

Outsourcing backlash?

It may be too small to be called a backlash, but a growing number of U.S. companies are having second thoughts about outsourcing. A question that seemed unthinkable in 2004 was being whispered in corporate conference rooms in 2005:

Is it really cheaper to outsource to China?

Shipping products to the United States from China is draining the savings made from lower salaries. For KenSa, frequent engineering changes insisted upon by the Big Three can make wire harnesses obsolete by the time they reach the U.S.

"We can put them on a boat and by the time they reach the United States, there have been two engineering changes," Zaima said.

In some cases, suppliers relocated in China have had to fly planeloads of re-engineered parts to the United States to avoid shutdowns of assembly lines, costing thousands more than it would have cost to ship by sea.

"If you take the supply chain and expand it by thousands of miles, it's not going to work as it's written on paper," said Jim

Applegate, an executive with National Logistics Management, a Detroit-based product transportation company.

C. Peter Theut, a trade attorney specializing in outsourcing, refers to the "lemmings" that rushed to China "because somebody higher in the food chain had a gun to their head."

"If you're just going for the labor costs, that's not a wise decision," Theut said. Many Chinese factory workers are the children of peasant farmers and have no background in factory skills. Many locations don't have reliable, 24-hour electricity.

"We bought the story that the OEMs (original equipment manufacturers) were selling to us more than we should have," Zaima said. OEMs that a year earlier prodded suppliers to move to China were in 2005 fretting over those same moves. "The OEMs say, 'You're not going to source this to China, are you?'" Zaima said.

The same reservations were being expressed in 2005 by some American customer service companies that moved call centers to India, with companies saying that the cost savings were offset by customer complaints.

For example, in 2005, cell phone provider Cingular Wireless was in the process of moving all its customer service centers back to the U.S. from Canada and India.

"It's a very complex decision to determine where facilities are placed, but we think all customer-care facilities should be in the United States," a Cingular spokesperson told the *Boston Globe*.

KenSa backed out of purchasing the factory and instead formed what amounts to an exclusive subcontractor relationship with the plant. Zaima still expects to import parts from China someday, but he's over his infatuation with the country and its low-wage workers.

Zaima's instincts proved right in July 2005 when China, which had manipulated the value of its currency for a decade to make its exports artificially cheap, changed its monetary policy.

Since 1985, one U.S. dollar has been worth about 8.3 yuan, the Chinese currency. Economists believed the yaun was undervalued by about 20 percent, meaning products produced in China and exported to the U.S. were 20 percent cheaper than their fair market value.

For China, the policy fueled a manufacturing boom, as the world clamored for the country's cheap products.

Many of those cheap products found their way into the shopping carts of American consumers. Wal-Mart, for example, which as recently as the early 1990s boasted of its policy to "Buy American," doubled its imports from China between 1998 and 2002. In 2002 alone, Wal-Mart stocked its shelves with about $12 billion in merchandise manufactured in China—nearly 10 percent of all Chinese exports to the United States

American consumers benefitted from a policy instituted by the Chinese government, even while some of them lost jobs because of that same policy.

Pegging the yuan to the value of the U.S. dollar made it even tougher for U.S. manufacturers to compete with Chinese factories. But it also provided an opportunity to American businesses willing to relocate half a world away.

Factories paid workers in undervalued yuan. The products those workers made could be sold in the U.S. cheaper because of the exchange rate.

Under intense pressure from the United States and other industrial nations, China in July 2005 began to allow its currency to fluctuate within limits with the world markets, as the currencies of most nations do. The yuan dropped 2 percent in value in the proceeding weeks, and experts expected it to drop more over the next few years.

"Everyone who migrated to China will make less money," Zaima said. "If you're importing to North America, you can go broke saving money."

Much of the production in China by U.S. auto supply companies is currently used in Chinese assembly plants for Chinese consumers. But the amount of auto parts imported from China for assembly in the U.S. was expected to increase exponentially in the next decade.

While U.S. companies are still moving to China, industry experts say momentum has slowed. "Companies that were pressured overseas are starting to look at the actual costs," said Kim Hill, of the Center for Automotive Research. "When you add everything up, are you getting the part cheaper than you would here? I think there is a real question."

The stronger yuan could further dampen enthusiasm for China outsourcing. But will China's loss be a gain for workers in the United States, Canada and Western Europe?

Probably not.

Searching for the next China
Zaima shied away from China because of concerns about shipping costs and logistics. The strengthening of the yuan in relation to the dollar made China even less attractive. But there are plenty of other countries out there without the headaches of China or the costs of the United States.

"Looking in the crystal ball, Honduras is our bread and butter," Zaima said. "There's a role for Mexico. And China will work if you have the right part."

What about the United States?

No way.

KenSa would be broke if it had kept its factories in Michigan, Zaima said.

Even Canada, an hour's boat trip across Lake Huron from Ken-Sa's former factory in Harbor Beach, is more attractive to industry than the United States.

In the summer of 2005, Toyota announced plans to build an assembly plant in Ontario. Many states offered Toyota more incentives to locate within their boundaries than did Ontario. But Canada offered something that no municipality in the Unites States could: national health insurance.

All Canadians have a basic level of health insurance provided by the government through taxes. Because the basics are covered, supplemental insurance offered to workers by some employers is much cheaper than the health insurance offered to workers in the United States. Thus, companies pay far less per employee in insurance costs. For a large assembly plant, the savings can be substantial.

In the U.S., insurance is the second-leading employee cost, next to wages. As an example, a worker earning $18,000 a year (about $10 an hour) could cost his employer an additional $12,000 a year for insurance for the worker and his family.

"That's why the Big Three are crying about insurance costs," Zaima said. A company could pay workers in Canada the equivalent salary of workers in the United States and still save money, because of the difference in insurance costs.

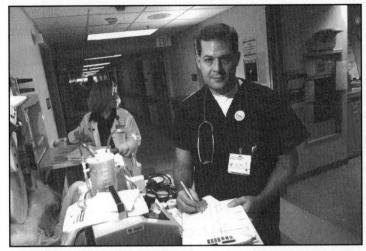

*Scott Caldwell at his new job. The former factory rat is training
to be a registered nurse, a career he feels will give him the
job security he no longer believes is possible in American factories.
Caldwell's factory job was moved to Canada in 2001.*

In developing countries, health care costs for companies are virtually nonexistent. In Mexico and Honduras, citizens have some basic health care paid for by the government, though Zaima adds that he's seen clinics in Honduras and doesn't recommend going there. KenSa's only expense is a full-time nurse at the plant, plus a doctor who visits the plant twice a week.

Companies are required by labor laws in Mexico and Honduras to have a medical professional at their factories during work hours.

In China, companies are not required to provide nurses, doctors or health insurance.

It's hard for Hardy to work up much sympathy. "The unemployed (American workers) don't have insurance either," he said.

EPILOGUE

Manufacturing isn't just increasingly global—it's increasingly dynamic. It's a jigsaw puzzle in which the pieces change shape in the blink of an eye. Workers and nations can change from winners to losers overnight.

If I've learned anything from following the production of wire harnesses across the globe, it's that we're all beneficiaries and victims of globalization. To believe the movement of jobs from industrialized nations to developing countries is only good or only bad is simplistic and unconstructive.

Workers in the United States, Canada, Japan and Western Europe are losing jobs to globalization while saving money on products made by their replacements in Indonesia, Haiti and the Czech Republic.

Company owners are saving millions of dollars by moving jobs overseas, while struggling with communication and cultural gaps with their employees.

We're all winners, we're all losers, and we'd all better get used to it. No one can put the genie back in the bottle. Offshoring of jobs is here to stay. And it's changing more than the price of our cars. Outsourcing is an economic reality, but the workers of KenSa illustrate that it's a social and cultural reality, too.

Consider just a few of the unexpected consequences of globalization:

• Outsourcing is contributing to a seismic shift in worker loyalty. The loss of good-paying factory jobs to Central America and Asia and the move of thousands of white-collar jobs to India has changed the social dynamics of the American workplace, said University of Michigan professor Richard Price. "The expectation used to be if the company takes care of me, I owe a certain amount of loyalty to the company," Price said. "That feeling is gone, especially among younger workers."

• Along the U.S.-Mexican border, outsourcing has increased the flow of legal and illegal immigrants. Hundreds of thousands of Mexicans have migrated from the impoverished southern region of the country to Mexican border towns to work in foreign-owned factories. Natives of the nation's poorest states, such as Oaxaca, Veracruz and Durango, continue to poor into border towns like Juárez while jobs are declining. Meanwhile, the buying power of the Mexican peso has plummeted, leaving even those with jobs struggling to survive. The employed and unemployed can look across the Rio Grande and see jobs that pay much more. Given a choice between traveling 1,000 miles back to their impoverished homeland or one mile to the United States, many more are sneaking across the border.

An estimated 3 million Mexicans cross into the United States illegally every year. Many go back and forth regularly, but some come north to stay.

Thus, outsourcing is not only costing American factory workers jobs, but also increasing the number of people looking for jobs in America.

• In Central America, maquiladoras are changing the social structure of families. Tens of thousands of women in Guatemala, El Salvador and Honduras are entering the formal workforce for the first time. "It's given women some independence," said Schrank, the Latin American sociologist from Yale. As women become empowered economically, they also become empowered in their traditionally male-dominated families.

"There is a high correlation between women's empowerment and fertility decline, infant mortality decline and more money being spent for children's education," Schrank said. Women make up the majority of workers in Central American factories such as the one owned by KenSa. Their jobs may do little to lift their families out of poverty, but their increased power in their families could help the next generation by increasing the emphasis on health and schools.

• In China, plants like the one where Huang formerly worked are sparking a new cultural revolution, and no one seems sure where it will lead. Millions are moving from farms to factories looking for a better life.

Some villages are virtually empty except for the elderly, leaving no one to work the fields. Cities are growing faster than leaders can figure out what to do with them.

Communist leaders of China are working furiously to build the infrastructure of roads and utilities needed to support foreign-owned factories, but are less sure-footed about the social costs.

"China has to deal with how to make these people upwardly

mobile," said Gallagher, the University of Michigan professor in Shanghai. "What about schools for their kids? Health care?"

Perhaps those aren't burning issues for 20-year-olds straight from the rice farm. But those 20-year-olds will have children someday. Those children will need schools, and their parents will need jobs that pay enough to support a family.

Already in Guangdong province, a region known as the "world's factory" that borders Hong Kong, some workers are refusing to take $50-a-month jobs, creating labor shortages.

• In Europe, outsourcing could save democracy in struggling former communist bloc nations. Countries that served as the Soviet Union's factories were left with shuttered plants when they declared independence.

Slovakia is a good example. Part of Czechoslovakia under the Soviet Union, Slovakia and the Czech Republic split into two independent nations in 1993. Slovakia had been the center of the old Soviet Union's defense industry. When it split from the Soviet Union, the economy went into a freefall. The new government wasn't communist, but it wasn't exactly democratic, either. Unemployment was high and political unrest was rampant.

Today, Slovakia is the fourth fastest-growing economy in the 25-nation European Union. Its capital, Bratislava, bills itself as "New Detroit," and it's easy to see why. Ford pledged in 2004 to invest $2.2 billion in Slovakia, where wages and taxes are even lower than in neighboring outsourcing destination the Czech Republic.

Peugeot's new 700 million-euro ($910 million U.S.) plant in Slovakia will, when completed, ship 300,000 cars a year to customers across Europe. Peugot picked Slovakia over Poland, where wages are low by Western Europe standards, but still 50 percent higher than Slovakia.

U.S. President George W. Bush praised Slovaks in a February 2005 trip to Bratislava, saying their development of a free market should be a model for other countries seeking democratic rule.

Slovak factory workers earn an average of $113 per week—a seventh of the wages of factory workers in Germany.

Slovakia, with 5.4 million inhabitants, could become the world's biggest car producer per capita by 2007, when car production is expected to reach almost 800,000 vehicles.

"The car industry needs skilled labor and Slovakia has it," Ludovit Ujhelyi, executive vice president of Slovakia's Automotive Industry Association, told Bloomberg News. He expects employment in the automotive industry to almost double to about 100,000 over the next five years.

Automakers Peugot and Renault have moved production from France to Slovakia. U.S. auto parts manufacturers Visteon, based in Michigan, and Johnson Controls, based in Wisconsin, are operating there or are building factories. Hankook Tire Company, a South Korean tiremaker and Japan's Denso Corporation, the world's third-largest maker of auto parts, were building plants in Slovakia in 2005.

What goes unsaid is that many of the jobs created in Slovakia represent jobs lost in Germany, France, Korea, Japan and the United States.

"The irony is that globalization is a product of U.S. successes," Will Marshall, president of the Progressive Policy Institute, said at an outsourcing conference in May 2005. "It was shaped by the collapse of socialism, the open trade policies of the 1990s, the exponentially growing power of IT (information technology) and the spread of high-speed Internet. We are living in a world we made—and many of us seem to be having second thoughts."

It likely will be left to our children to settle the debate over outsourcing. In 50 years, will the industrial upheaval we're experiencing today be considered the beginning of global parity, lifting hundreds of millions of third-world residents out of poverty? Will it be considered the end of the era of American domination? What will happen to the blue-collar middle class? Will we in first-world nations find other ways to maintain our lifestyles, or will we be left with no way to earn a paycheck but to deliver pizzas to each other?

"The truth is, someone's gotta do the dirty work in the economy," said Schrank, "and it tends to be people in former colonies of old European powers."

Maybe the Yale professor is right. Maybe the Deb Coverdills of the world will have to get used to a lower standard of living, a standard of living that, even after declaring bankruptcy, will probably always be higher than that of Huang Wei.

In 2004, Huang had something more precious to Coverdill than a paycheck. she had confidence. Huang believed no one could take her job. She believed her future in the factory was bright. She believed with the same surety and naivety which Coverdill had velt just a few years earlier.

In 2004, the two women shared a common job and boss.

In 2005, they shared only insecurity.

JUST THE FACTS

United States Facts

- *Population:* 293 million
- *Per capita income (in U.S. dollars, 2003):* $37,610
- *Percentage living in poverty:* 12%
- *Unemployment:* 6%
- *Labor force:* 146 million
- *Industrial labor force:* 35 million
- *Industrial production growth rate (2002–2003):* 0.3% (134th globally)
- *Infant mortality per 1,000 births:* 6.63
- Michigan has lost 51,000 jobs to Mexico and Canada in the past decade, and is expected to lose another 46,000 to offshoring by 2012.
- Manufacturing jobs are being replaced with jobs that pay less.
- The world's supply of cheap labor could last for centuries.
- Michigan workers may face lower wages and a lower standard of living.
- *Number of workers who can be hired for the pay of a KenSa worker in the U.S.:* 1 worker at $7.50 an hour.

Mexico Facts

- *Population:* 104 million
- *Per capita income* (in U.S. dollars, 2003): $5,910
- *Percentage living in poverty:* 40%
- *Unemployment:* 8%; underemployment: 20%
- *Labor force:* 34 million
- *Industrial labor force:* 8.1 million
- *Industrial production growth rate (2002–2003):* -1.07% (149th globally)
- *Infant mortality per 1,000 births:* 21.69
- About 700 of the Fortune 1000 companies operate in Mexico.
- Foreign-owned factories in Mexico grew from 160 in 1970 to 3,200 in 2002.
- Wages and benefits for workers have gone up.
- Forty percent of the nation continues to live in poverty.
- Some factories leave for cheaper markets, costing some workers their jobs.
- *Number of workers who can be hired for the pay of a KenSa worker in the U.S.:* 5.5 workers at $1.35 an hour.

Honduras Facts

- *Population:* 6.8 million
- *Per capita income (in U.S. dollars, 2003):* $930
- *Percentage living in poverty:* 53%
- *Unemployment:* 28%
- *Labor force:* 2.4 million
- *Industrial labor force:* 504,000
- *Industrial production growth rate (2002–2003):* 7.7% (36th globally)
- *Infant mortality per 1,000 births:* 29.64
- Honduras is the size of Ohio but has the third-largest number of foreign-owned factories in the world.
- The per-capita income of Hondurans is $930, with a purchasing power half that of Chinese workers and less than a third that of Mexican workers.
- Fifty-five-cent-per-hour jobs are attractive in an economy with a 28 percent jobless rate.
- Factory pay isn't sufficient to lift workers out of poverty.
- *Number of workers who can be hired for the pay of a KenSa worker in the U.S.:* 9.2 workers at 81¢ an hour.

China Facts

- *Population:* 1.3 billion
- *Per capita income (in U.S. dollars, 2003):* $1,450
- *Percentage living in poverty:* 10%
- *Unemployment:* 20%
- *Labor force:* 778 million
- *Industrial labor force:* 171 million
- *Industrial production growth rate (2002–2003):* 30.4% (1st globally)
- *Infant mortality per 1,000 births:* 25.28
- Industrial production in China is growing faster than in any other nation—up 30 percent from 2002 to 2003.
- Ford, GM and DaimlerChrysler are rushing into China to get a piece of a burgeoning Chinese auto market. The Big Three encourage auto part makers to go to China to supply their factories.
- Auto supplier factories in China can produce parts for less money because the average salary is about 50 cents an hour.
- U.S. factories must match the price of Chinese-made auto parts, move to China, or go out of business.
- *Number of workers who can be hired for the pay of a KenSa worker in the U.S.:* 16.7 workers at 45¢ an hour.

ACKNOWLEDGMENTS

This book, and stories on the same subject published in *The Detroit News*, would not have been possible without the support and encouragement of Mark Silverman, publisher and editor of *The Detroit News*. Mark shared my enthusiasm and vision for this project, and found money in a tight budget to send photographer Max Ortiz and me jetting around the globe to report it.

Thanks must also go to Don Nauss, whose guidance helped refine my often jumbled ideas, and who always pushed to make it better, rather than publish it faster; to Mark Truby, who provided masterful editing and invaluable insights into the auto industry; and to Laura Berman for her encouragement and creativity. As she has throughout my career, my wife, Valerie von Frank, provided dead-on criticism, excellent copyediting and heaping portions of patience.

This book would not have been the same without Max Ortiz, whose photos capture the spirit of the workers with whom we visited. A Max Ortiz photo is definitely worth a thousand Ron French words.

Richard Hollingham in London and Jiri Nadoba in Prague provided invaluable assistance in understanding how outsourcing is affecting Europe.

Qian "Flora" Yu, our translator and guide in China, was a God-send, helping us understand our very foreign surroundings.

And finally, a special thanks to Hal Zaima, John Clough and John Nye of KenSa LLC. They courageously opened up their business and their lives to a journalist even as they shipped American jobs overseas. They believed, as I did, that their story was a story that had to be told.

ABOUT THE AUTHOR

As a senior writer at *The Detroit News,* Ron French has covered some of the major news events of the past two decades. He has written about terrorism and presidential politics, flooding along the Mississippi and the execution of Timothy McVeigh. In 2000, his series on how lax oversight of collegiate study abroad programs led to the murder of two American women in Costa Rica sparked a Congressional investigation. In 2001, three years unraveling problems in a Detroit murder investigation culminated with the release of a man wrongly imprisoned for 15 years.

French has won dozens of journalism awards. He was granted a prestigious Knight-Wallace Fellowship at the University of Michigan in 2002-03, where he was the Mike Wallace Investigative Journalism Fellow.

A graduate of Purdue University, French lives in Okemos, Michigan, with his wife, two daughters and an assortment of pets.